Voices of The Potteries

The source of the Trent, Biddulph near Hanley.

Stoke-on-Trent 'Always Merry and Bright'.

Voices of The Potteries

Alan Taylor

First published in 2001 by Tempus Publishing

Reprinted in 2009 by
The History Press
The Mill, Brimscombe Port,
Stroud, Gloucestershire, GL5 2QG
www.thehistorypress.co.uk

Reprinted 2013

Copyright © Alan Taylor, 2001

ISBN 978 0 7524 2276 3

Typesetting and origination by
Tempus Publishing Limited
Printed in Great Britain.

Dedication

For Jan, Josh and Sam

Acknowledgements

I would like to thank all the contributors to this book. They have given generously of their time and their memories. As always it is a great pleasure and a great privilege to be admitted so warmly into the lives of so many. In particular I want to thank Eveline Shore whose generosity of spirit as well as of memory is an example to us all.

I must also thank those who have provided photographs. Many images in this volume have not been published before and, like the words, they throw a unique light on the history of the Potteries.

This book is written in memory of Fred Leigh.

Contents

Acknowledgements		4
Introduction		6
1.	Growing Up	11
2.	Leisure	27
3.	War Years and Beyond	62
4.	Work	77

Burslem Town Hall.

Introduction

Stoke-on-Trent is a particular mixture of identities. The city of today was created in 1925 but the foundations were laid in no less than six towns over the preceding generations. The boroughs of Longton, Hanley, Stoke and Burslem, and the urban districts of Fenton and Tunstall formed the County Borough of Stoke-on-Trent in 1910. Each town had its own identity, a sense of which still persists today although inevitably in a diluted form. Ask anybody from the city where they are from and they will specifically tell you Fenton, Birches Head, Heron Cross or Longport. They rarely say Stoke-on-Trent, even when on holiday in Australia. The local culture has been enriched with those cultures of people from Asia, Poland, Ireland and Wales to name but a few.

By the time of the earliest memories recorded in this book, the Potteries was already a heavily industrialized area. Unique in the country for being named after its principle industry, the nomenclature is nonetheless misleading. The whole is the sum of its parts, and Stoke in addition to all the minor industries, had three major sources of wealth and employment.

Firstly there was the mining industry. Coal was the real reason behind the pottery industry being located in this northern part of the Midlands. There were and still are, vast deposits of coal in the north Staffordshire coal fields, coal of an extremely high quality, ideal for burning in the potters' kilns. Pits were sunk everywhere. There is evidence of mining for coal from at least the second century AD. The cutting of the Trent and Mersey Canal in 1777 opened up the coal industry in Stoke to the national economy as it did the pottery industry. As output increased to meet demand the number of individual collieries declined as smaller enterprises merged with larger or were forced into closure by fluctuations in the market. By the time of the 1984-85 strike, there were nearly 6,000 miners employed at the Hem Heath, Florence, Silverdale, Holditch and Wolstanton pits. The year-long strike was often bitterly fought in north Staffordshire. The strikers established a new sense of community as families and neighbourhoods united in a common struggle to save jobs. The North Staffordshire Miners' Wives Action Group was particularly active in raising funds for families, attending rallies, keeping the strike in the public eye. It was they who commissioned a sculpture that now stands in The Potteries Museum & Art Gallery. During the course of the 1980s however, the fears of the miners' leaders were realised and the pits closed. Today there are no working pits in the coal field. A final and sad legacy is that the underground workings continue to subside.

Pot banks sprang up alongside or near to mines making the two industries interdependent. Local coal was of a high quality and was extracted in vast quantities. Only with the introduction of electric kilns and the clean air acts was the direct relationship broken. In addition to the large internationally famous names in the industry, numerous smaller pot banks sprang up throughout the city providing generations of families with a living. The pot bank became the focus of life for many. People literally lived next door to their place of work.

Times Square and Longton Town Hall, c. 1900.

Wedgwood attempted a model village with Etruria, building houses for his work force but failing to provide the facilities and services required. In other areas such as John Street, the poor living conditions proved a trap from which people could not escape until they were re-housed by the local authority. But while the pottery industry contributed to the poor health of the population, the likes of Wedgwood and Spode subscribed to the North Staffordshire Infirmary which was the first hospital in the area to provide health care for the working classes. The workers themselves were also encouraged to subscribe at the rate of a farthing or a penny a week. By the time of the creation of the National Health Service in 1948, there were over 150,000 subscribers to the area's voluntary hospitals.

During the late nineteenth century the north Staffordshire iron and steel industries rapidly expanded. Quality steel was produced at Shelton from the 1840s and by the 1920s, 9,000 tons of steel and iron were produced each week. Wages at Shelton were higher than those in the pottery industry making the plant a more attractive employment option, although like all other industries Shelton bar was hit by world recession. On 27 April 2000, the last length of steel went through the rolling mill.

These industries, never environmentally friendly, had a devastating impact on the local landscape. Open-cast mining, marl pits and waste tips dominated the area. As factories grew and the population expanded, increasing demands were put on the blighted green spaces between the six towns of Tunstall, Burslem, Hanley, Stoke, Fenton and Longton. Terrace upon terrace of workers' houses were erected literally on the doorsteps of pot banks. Generations of potters went to work for the same company as their forebears and the loyalty to firms is still apparent today. They spent long hours working in cramped conditions, often with noxious substances and inhaling the smoke of the kilns. The stunted bottle ovens, never designed to carry airborne waste away from the immediate area, deposited thick layers of dust in the houses and at firing up times blocked the sun's light from the streets. The city's health statistics still reveal the legacy of the excessive levels of pollution that were not addressed until the clean air acts of the 1950s.

Although the canals and road systems allowed easier import and export of goods to and from the region, it was the coming of the railways that reduced costs and allowed industrial development to really accelerate. By mid-1849 negotiations between numerous local concerns allowed for the establishment of the North Staffordshire Railway which served several purposes. Firstly it provided a passenger transport network. Secondly it provided transport for the iron and steel industry as well as the pottery industry. Thirdly it linked the city to the growing national railway system. The company operated its own locomotive and rolling stock construction and maintenance depot that employed about a thousand people. It also ran its own hotels of which the North Stafford opposite Stoke Station is perhaps the finest example. The company also owned the canal system, thus effectively controlling any competition. Known affectionately as The Knotty, the NSR continued to operate up until a takeover by the LMS and ultimately nationalization.

The following interviews do not dwell on these principle industries however. Others are working in these areas and the subjects deserve books in their own right. The current volume seeks to portray a side of the Potteries away from the typical and the stereotypical. The simple chapter structure reflects a diversity of life. A core of interviewees from different walks of life was

The impact of large scale excavations at Trent Vale.

chosen to focus more on the aspects of daily living and to hopefully reveal something of the character of being a potter.

Within this book we read of people going about their work and their play. There is a richness of life underlying even the gloomiest of the heavily polluted days. Many of the interviewees spoke of the weekend trip out of the city into the countryside by bike, train or car. Obviously then, as now, escaping the routine of everyday life was important. Others spoke affectionately of their trips to the cinema or to the dance hall, particularly during the war years. The influence of foreign nationals and evacuees, albeit temporarily lodged in the city, must have been a great boost to local people. There is an openess about courting and relationships. The infamous monkey runs are a fascinating study in popular and youth culture. What is missing however, is the unique Potteries dialect. For many now, the dialect is something of the past. Unfortunate as this may be, it has made transcribing the interviews easier!

These are issues for which little or no material evidence survives. Much sadly passes away with those who lived the experience and it is the *experience*, spoken of first hand, that is important. This is the value of oral history and books such as this. Oral history is often devalued as being unreliable, but taken in tandem with other sources of information; it enriches our understanding of the past. It also empowers people to investigate and ultimately express their own sense of historical and cultural identity.

During the course of my research for this book, one interviewee, Roger Brown, who is admittedly a newcomer to the area, summarised something of the character of the city and its people:

'I work at Staffordshire University as Senior Lecturer of Photography in the School of Art and Design. I moved here because of my job from Charlbury, Oxfordshire in 1989. It was not a move I wanted to make. I had commuted for three years since 1986 but that became untenable. Since then I have remarried to a Newcastle-born woman, served four years as a Liberal Democrat councillor on Newcastle Borough Council and feel quite settled. There is much that I like about the place and the people, especially the people, and naturally things I am less keen on.

There is an openness, honesty and frankness to people here that I like very much. I'm not much impressed by people who flaunt themselves, their money or their status. People don't do that here generally. They take you at face value for what you are, what you can do, look you in the eye and respect that. They ask only for the same in return. There is a quality of selflessness and toleration that, oddly enough, shows itself in the way people drive. I know of nowhere else where people are so willing to stop and let you out in front of them, even if they are on the main road and you are on a side road. I used to think it infuriating, dangerous and often barmy. Not now. Now I think it graceful and courteous. Elsewhere people drive with a 'me first at all costs' attitude, and that selfishness shows in other aspects of their lives too as a greed and self-centredness. Perhaps it is a northern thing; my wife tells me it is. As a southerner I certainly notice the difference between here and the Home Counties.'

Roger Brown, born 1945

Bagnall Cross, written on the back is 'Don't you think it is pretty?'

CHAPTER 1
Growing Up

Oak Hill, Stoke-on-Trent.

The people interviewed each had different experiences of childhood and early adulthood. This chapter reflects this diversity. It begins with one person's recollections of moving to the area from one in which cultural intolerance predominated. The family moved to an area in which numerous families lived below the bread line and in what we would term squalor. Despite the harsh conditions endured by Potteries families, the most was made of everything around them. Children learnt to play on the wastelands, their imagination allowed to run riot before the need to earn extra money pressed them into finding jobs on leaving school. Those days at school, often anecdotally described as the best of our lives, were viewed as strict and the teachers authoritarian, but with hindsight also a degree of fairness.

Jewish Faith

My parents came from Lithuania to this country because of oppression, Pogroms. It was dangerous to be a Jew and live in that area and my father had some connection with somebody in Germany who assisted his passage. He landed in the port of Hull I believe and made his way cross country earning a living by selling various articles as he went along. And then he was assisted by somebody in South Wales, who had children who were brought up in the Jewish faith and my father was rather learned in the Jewish faith. And he taught them Hebrew, and then from there he went on, on his way, on his travels, and I think he met his wife, my mother, in Manchester, where they were married, and they came to live in what was in those days not the City of Stoke-on-Trent, but just the area of Stoke-on-Trent it hadn't become a city until 1924 I believe. They settled in Hope Street where my father began a varied career first of all as a cycle repair shop owner and then later as a coal merchant delivering coal with a horse and wagon and then he took up scrap metal collection. My brother became a commercial traveller and later on he entered the family scrap business which had by then increased a great deal. He served in the army but I think he had a discharge through illness and my two sisters, they had stalls in the markets selling cloth and drapery. I remember when I was very young being afraid of local people who hated Jews and on one occasion one of them broke a window and threatened a whole family. I remember running along with my father to find a policeman to give us protection. That's the oldest recollection I have of anti-Semitism in that area.

Sam Singer, born 1911

Humble Beginnings

I was born in North Road, Cobridge of very humble people. At the age of two my father died and my mother had to sell the little house for the funeral. From then onwards we were pushed in anybody's house. We had no home at all. There was my mother, my sister and my brother. We had no food, no clothes, nothing. We used to have parish bread. We had no money to buy bread. The parish gave us a house down Granville's building in Cobridge and we slept there only one night, in the toilet, because it was alive with vermin.

Elizabeth Stringer, born 1904

Earliest Memories

My earliest memories of my parents were when we moved from Far Green down to Northwood. I think I was round about seven. I had another brother who was five, another brother who was fourteen, me mother and me father. We hadn't got much money and we moved from Far Green on a pram, believe it or not, down to Keelings Road. We lived in Keelings Road from around about 1942 up to 1956 when I went in the forces. We finished up with eight children, mother and father. Me mother left home when I was about twelve, which left me father in charge of eight kids. He died at the age of forty-seven with a heart attack which is not surprising.

Roy Furnival, born 1936

First Bathroom

My earliest memories of my childhood; I had an Irish mother who was only a very slightly built lady with a typical Irish temper and a very placid, easy going father. I was born to them late in life. My mother was forty-four and my dad was about forty-eight. I'd got two brothers, George who was nine years older than me and Norman who's six years older than me. We were middle of the road class wise I would say. My father had got a job as a kiln fireman on Twyford's and he used to earn quite a reasonable wage. We were the first people in Cliffe Vale, the first family in Gower Street in Cliffe Vale, to have a bathroom built, so everyone came along to have a look at our bathroom. I was really that chuffed with the bathroom, I used to take magazines in there and chocolate biscuits and drinks of pop. All me biscuits used to melt in the bath.

Rhona Atkins, born 1938

Clothes

When I was a kid I was the third eldest, there was another five below me. We used to go to the WVS in Stoke opposite Oak Church to get our clothes. I can remember one outfit I had from there. I can see it plain as day now. They were blue suede shoes, brown check trousers and a Canadian black and white lumber jacket and I had to walk around in them and go to school in them. And I can remember we used to have to go down to the cinder tip where the corporation place was built down Cromer Road, and we used to find old jumpers and we used to cut the sleeves out at the corners from corner to corner and sew them up and use them for socks. Then I remember once me father must have had a windfall and he bought me a new shirt. It was a lovely pale blue shirt and I was so proud of it. I was walking up the side of Northwood Park one day when I'd got this shirt on and I remembered some of the lads there were some of the rough lads at school. If you went to school really posh and clean they'd pick on you. So I remember putting my hands on the floor to get some dirt on and rubbed it down my shirt so that when I got to school the kids wouldn't actually say anything about me being posh!

Roy Furnival, born 1936

Trentham Park

My only real memory of Trentham Park as a child was sitting on the edge of the pool trying to ignore the numerous insects floating in the water, including a large still living wasp. There seemed an awful lot of rubbish in the water, but it's the insects – especially the wasp – which I remember most vividly. Obviously not a very happy memory of childhood, but it was sad being in the area with the Deer Survey some twenty years later and seeing the place completely derelict and vandalized.

Steve Crompton, born 1956

Captain Smith

I am a direct descendant of Captain Smith. I have several personal effects of his but nothing off the *Titanic* apart from a lump of coal! My father remembered Captain Smith, he used to go into my grandfather's pub on odd occasions. Dad always referred to him as Uncle John and I knew his daughter. She died in 1972. Simon the son, was a Beaufighter pilot and he got killed in 1944, I think it was the 23 March 1944. He was shot down off the Norwegian coast.

The swimming pool at Trentham Gardens.

Captain Smith's wife got knocked down by a taxi in 1930 and was killed and the taxi driver's name was Robert Smith.

Don Smith, born 1939

The Jewish Community

Many Jews have left Stoke to get more in the way of opportunities in the bigger cities and all sorts of difficulties of finding a suitable spouse. If you were a Jew, a male Jew, in those days looking for a female obviously you didn't believe in what was called exogamy which means marrying out. If you married out in some ways it was disgraceful because you gave up your religion and your progeny would be half and half. They wouldn't know which way to turn either to Christianity on the mother's side or Judaism on the father's side and there are many cases of that happening. It's going on today, I believe fifty percent throughout England now are marrying what they call 'out'.

Sam Singer, born 1911

It's Where You Grew Up

My mother and father lived in Hanley, St John's Street, where I was born and soon after we went to Stone and lived in Stone until I was six. Then we came back to Shelton and lived in Grove Lodge which was opposite the Bell and Bear. The Bell and Bear is still there but the lodge has been pulled down. I can remember my mother telling me that the noise were dreadful, it was a very noisy town. Stone was very quiet and select while Shelton and Hanley, they were dirty, sooty, horrible. We had a big garden but because the atmosphere was bad with the soot and the dirt nothing would grow. So the only thing we had was, I think, was a poplar tree, a horse chestnut tree. We had a tennis court. The only things that we could grow were Michaelmas Daisies and a few bedding plants. But autumn came very quickly in the town and about June all the leaves fell off the trees because of the soot. Plants, well we had plants for about six weeks then they died.

Angela Mellor, born 1915

Shop Keepers

All the shop keepers in Etruria were friendly with each other and many experiences were shared. Down in the village there was Mr Shearer the printer who was in the Salvation Army. Florrie Ball kept a fish and chip shop and there was a butcher's shop kept by Mr Palmer. On the main road going towards Hanley there was Mrs Quinn the outdoor beer retailer; she also sold Kali and gob stoppers. Then there was Mr Barnes the pawnbroker; many bargains could be had at his shop. Articles which had not been reclaimed were eventually sold for a reasonable price. Mr Barnes was a regimental type of gentleman. He would tell the boys passing by to hold their backs up and call out like a sergeant major 'Left, right!' Mr Harry Knowles and his sister Mrs Ford both had mixed business shops. A little further up the road was a small slaughterhouse and butcher's shop belonging to Mr Palmer. Here you could see black puddings being made. In Cavendish Street, there was a fish and chip shop run by Mr and Mrs Mansell. The son of the family was naturally called 'Chippy' though his real name was Herbert. They must have been very prosperous, they were one of the fortunate few who could take a week's holiday at the seaside each year. The only holiday most of the children had was when they went on the Sunday school trip. The trip was mostly to the seaside resort of Rhyl in north Wales. This trip usually took place the week after the Sunday school festival. Children who had attended the Sunday school for most of the year went free. On the festival day the children would put on their best clothes and parade around the streets.

Eveline Shore, born 1919

Blacked Out

I do remember playing in the street and when there was a down draught of air from one of the ovens, and the nearest one to us would be Meakins, the Eagle Works, and being absolutely blacked out. Just instantaneously, and you could not see who you were with. It was like being in black cotton wool. The funny thing is I don't remember smelling it, because you must have smelt it all your life. Only when I was coming back in the '50s, into the city via the train, when you drew into Stoke did you smell the atmosphere for just a second or two and then you got accustomed to it.

Graham Davies, born 1930

Cock Sparrow Hall

For a few years I worked as a home help and if possible I would finish my duties early so that I could have a chat and maybe a cup of coffee with my clients. On one such occasion I was talking to an elderly lady who I had met the previous week. She asked me where I was born and when I told her that I had been born in a small cottage

Fresh air from the Potteries!

in Springfields, she said, 'You weren't born in Cock Sparrow Hall were you?' I had heard the cottage called that before, but we called it Hawthorn Cottage which was a prettier name. It turned out that she had been born at the same cottage about three years before me. I was interested to know what the cottage was like when she and her family lived there. It transpired that the cottage had tragic memories for her. She was the eldest child of a gentleman who was the gardener at the London Road Hospital and workhouse. She had a sister who was a year younger than herself and her mother was expecting another child. There was a deep pond at the back of the cottage and during play the little sister fell into the water. Telling her to stay where she was, her mother went into the water to save the sister but tragically both were drowned. Shortly after, the father and child moved.

On a lighter note I remember my mother telling me of the time when there were some youths larking about the pond and one fell in. They came to our house and mother found him some old clothes of my dad's to go home in. It was only later my mother found out that they were trying to steal our ducks.

The garden was very large. There were two huge lilac trees which formed a bower of sweet scented blooms in the early spring. At each side of the path were beds of sweet alyssum, ten week stocks, asters of all colours and old fashioned garden pinks, and then a rockery of pretty flowers. To the right of the green wicket gate was our privy, concealed by glossy green ivy.

The cottage was warm and cosy with a red quarry floor, a window furnished with pretty flowered curtains and a bright red fire burning in the blackened range. There was not a lot of furniture. A sofa which had seen better days was on one side of the fireplace and a large easy chair to the other side. A large white scrubbed kitchen table and four dining chairs were in the centre of the kitchen. In the corner of the room was a round mahogany table covered with chenille cloth. On the table was our only lighting, a large brass lamp with a tall glass cover about two feet in height. It had a tiered base which for some reason did not stand level. I remember it had to be made level by placing a folded newspaper to one side.

We didn't have the luxury of a bathroom with hot and cold water. All we had was a cold water tap in the kitchen. Yet having a wash or a bath was always a pleasant occasion. Each morning dad used to get up early and light the coal fire. The large black kettle would be put on. The first thing dad did was to make a pot of tea and take a cup upstairs to mum in bed. Then we would take turns to go to wash in the kitchen. I never felt cold in the kitchen. I would have a large enamel bowl filled with warm weather and it was so pleasant to dip my arms into the lovely warm water before lathering with carbolic soap. Bath nights in the winter were taken in the front bedroom where we could bath in private.

Eveline Shore, born 1919

Old White Hill

I was seven years of age when we went to live in Old White Hill in the early 1950s. We lived there for only two years, I did not return to the area until comparatively recently but this strange and bleak place has had a powerful impact on my life.

The village comprised a square of sixteen rambling houses built in the nineteenth

A view of a bottle oven and the bridge over the canal, with heavily polluted air ever-present.

century for employees from the Birchenwood Colliery. There was no made road leading to the village, only a farmer's muddy lane and paths through the fields. It was bleak in winter but a joy in summer. Slag heaps, thrown up from the colliery, formed vast and gloomy mountains which cast shadows across the houses and rugged landscape. Known locally as the Rucks, these mountains were ugly and ominous but we children loved climbing and playing on them. They became fantasy landscapes which intrigued and excited me by day and which troubled my dreams by night.

On the other side of the Rucks were the smoking chimneys and furnaces of the huge Birchenwood Colliery and Coking Plant. Surrounding the colliery was an inviting and strangely deserted world of pathways which wound through a hilly terrain dotted with giant cinders, smoldering ash beds, murky pools, reservoirs fenced off with barbed wire and abandoned railway lines overgrown with tall yellow grass and rose bay willow herb. It was a fascinating and compelling environment which provided us with endless days of wandering, imagination and adventure.

Val Kosh

Berry Hill

On Berry Hill one of the favourite places to play was the shard rucks which were the piles of waste from the pottery industry. I learnt later there were two types. There were the shard ruck and the shraff tip; I don't actually know the difference. The shard rucks we'd go and plunder for the plaster moulds which we used as chalk. But the main thing we looked for was what we called alley glass. This was the lining of the bottle ovens. If you can imagine the glaze would vapourise and over many years it would coat the inside with a skin of different coloured glazes. Regularly this would be chipped off and taken to the shard ruck. For young boys these lumps of coloured glass were quite fascinating. Alley glass was of great importance to us. We played alleys, we didn't play marbles. As young kids we would gather together in gangs. The gang was very important to young boys. We would actually catch the bus to places like Trentham and then walk to Beech Caves or to Bagnall to visit the woods or to Stanley to walk round the pool. We were quite adventurous; children nowadays don't seem to do that sort of thing. We would actually walk for a long, long way. Most of our playing was on Berry Hill while the coal mine was still working. My grandfather worked down Berry Hill pit as a platelayer and many a happy day we would be chased by the NCB bobby. The bonfires were amazing. We had the whole of the colliery area and the farmland to choose from, so we had huge bonfires of railway sleepers and cable drums. You name it we burnt it! We would go up into the farmland at Berry Hill and steal the chonnocks – which are turnips.

Andrew Harrison, born 1947

Canals

Alick and I and our family of four children moved up to Staffordshire in early 1968 because of Alick's job. I was a little bit gob smacked to begin with. We had a day out here to look around. With Alick's job being with Wedgwood we got the director's chauffeur to drive us around which was quite posh really! I thought it was quite nice, around the canals

A marl hole and shard ruck.

which I thought was lovely. We had Andrew our second son with us who was absolutely passionate about canals, but he'd only read about them in books. So that particular day we came up to look around and see the house we were going to live in which was the old Vic Skellern house on the Barlaston estate, he wouldn't come back with us. He wanted to wander around more and see more canals. When we got back to London he was so excited about living here, simply because of the canals.

Betty Smithers

Working Class

I come from a working class family in Brown Lees which is near Biddulph. The area was commonly known as the Huts. It was a road sandwiched between the ironworks and the railway sidings to the local pit, which was Victoria Pit, commonly known as Black Bull. Private, rented housing, terraced type of housing, two-up, two-down, outside toilet. There was just myself and my sister, mother and father. Our grandparents lived just across the road, uncle just down the road. My father was originally employed as what they called a wagon bodger which repaired the old railway wagons. He then went working down the pit.

My uncle also worked in the pit. He had six brothers and two sisters, three of which were down the pit, the others in local mills.

Charles Bibby, born 1955

In The Accent

The dialect we would have used, you weren't aware of because that was the way of saying things. When I was a child and with a practised ear, you could hear the difference of accent from Longton to Hanley to Tunstall and you could place people by their accent. I don't think you can now. I didn't consciously try to lose my accent but I think I've lost a lot of it. Even so, I was quite shocked in London to be pinpointed as someone from the north Midlands because *one can't hear one's own accent!* My brother lost his through work.

Andrew Harrison, born 1947

Stardom Beckons

Me and a friend of mine decided we were going to form our own band as you do at the age of about twelve. I bought my first guitar from a sort of combination of work over the summer and a birthday present. It was a horrible thing that you couldn't really play at all, but it was electric and from Chatfields, which sadly is closed now. Me and my friend, we both bought a guitar on the same day and decided to form a band called, we were all into punk stuff then, Broken Down Fence by a Skinhead in Doc Martins which we thought was really cool. So we had this school band and put on concerts. We couldn't play at all but we arranged this huge thing, saying that we were *the* school band. We were absolutely awful. We did versions of, and we really thought we could get away with it, we did a 45 minute version of 'Sister Ray' by the Velvet Underground which is only three chords as it is and is a complete noise all the way through. So we got up and did a 45-minute version of complete noise!

Crispin Hunt

Birthday Memories

I was born on September 8th, 1919. The large double bed would have been brought downstairs which was the practice in those days. I was delivered by the local midwife, Nurse Harvey from Trent Vale. In my layette, mum had included a tablet of Pears Golden Glory soap, the favourite soap in those days. Nurse Harvey declined to use it. 'There's nothing wrong with a bit of White Windsor' she said. My mother's old doctor, Doctor Webster, would also be present.

Eveline Shore, born 1919

Alton Towers

I have many memories of Alton Towers: I went every year on my birthday. A barber shop quartet sang 'Happy Birthday' to me in the middle of the theme park which was very embarrassing. Even when I was young I was tall enough to go on the big rides. The Corkscrew was the best ride in the whole park, and then the Pirate Ship. I used to get bored as my parents walked around the gardens. I remember liking the Chinese Pavilion when I saw it from the cable car. Once we dressed up in eighteenth-century costume to have our photograph taken. I liked to have my face painted too. It was the best day of the year. It was always sunny.

Liz Dawson, born 1977

The Longpigs, fronted by Crispin Hunt, play at The Wheatsheaf in Stoke.

Health

The earliest recollections of my life were when I had to go into the Haywood Hospital at about the age of three years to have my appendix removed. Whilst I was in there I remember my mum brought me some grapes and me and the lad in the next bed were eating these grapes and blowing the pips all over the floor for which we were told off in no uncertain terms by the matron. The stitches when they pulled them out were very painful but other than that, that is all I can remember about that episode.

Reg White, born 1929

Bubble Gum

Two things I liked and couldn't have. One was that pink bubble gum you blew bubbles with. I wasn't supposed to have that but naturally I loved the taste of it. I always remember being told if you swallowed it, it wrapped its way round your heart and you died. Somebody had given me a bit and I was chewing away enjoying it and I swallowed it. I remember going up and sat in the greenhouse in the back yard waiting to die. I remember this. This would be before I was six because we left that house and I sobbed my little heart out. I remember thinking I shan't see Mum and Dad anymore and I cried. I was thinking I shan't see my sister Elsie anymore and I cried and I thought I shan't see Grandma anymore though that didn't upset me too much! But I seemed to spend hours, but it was probably only fifteen minutes you know, and I didn't die. It was one of those little turning points in life when everything an adult tells you isn't right. I'd swallowed this piece of chewing gum definitely, and I had definitely not died!

Graham Davies, born 1930

Dreamlike

My earliest memory is of a dream, a dream remembering sun ray treatment when I was a child of about eighteen months old. I think the clinic was in Wellesley Street in Shelton. It was a very strange experience. We all sat around in a very dark room with a light shining and everyone wore goggles; it was very mysterious and dreamlike anyway. To a child it must have been quite scary.

Andrew Harrison, born 1947

School Days

The Sacred Heart School was in Jasper Street; it belonged to the Catholic Church. They used to have two classes, very often in one room. The teachers were back to back, a teacher taught one half of the class at one side of the room and the other teacher taught the class at the other side, but you could always hear what was going on. You had to pass in five subjects including grammar and literature and you had to read a book. You had to do arithmetic and you had to do one language.

Angela Mellor, born 1915

Trent Vale Infant School

It was in September 1924 that I started to attend Trent Vale Infant's School. It was in part of the Wesleyan chapel in Flash Lane. The first class was in a room where the desks were in stages. My first seat was near the back. On my first day I must have been tired and yawned. This brought tears to my eyes and the teacher, Miss Morris, thought I was crying. She called me to the front of the class and asked me if I would like to go home. Although I assured her that I was all right, she insisted that one of the older boys took me home when I really didn't want to. The boy she chose was Harold Snape, the son of our next door neighbour. Getting out of the schoolyard he promptly ran off to play.

Eveline Shore, born 1919

Glass Street School

I was one of the last lads to go to the Glass Street School in Hanley which in those days was for boys and girls. I didn't like school I must admit. Didn't like the teachers; they didn't like me. From there I went to Broom Street School when Glass Street became all girls. When I went to Broom Street I ended back in hospital with pneumonia and I was in there, the City General, for a month or two when I caught scarlet fever off one of the nurses. I was transferred to the Bucknall Isolation Hospital where I stopped for a fortnight while I got over the scarlet fever. Then I went back to school again. Through having these illnesses I was very fortunate in being excused having PT and this carried on all through the school. I never did it at school although it never stopped me running everywhere. But I thought it was good to watch all the other people jumping up and down.

Reg White, born 1929

Education

Unfortunately for me, my mother died when I was two, which left my father and my sister who was just six months old. So we went all through the 1930s as a one-parent family. When the war came the education system collapsed and when it did start up again we went to school either in the morning or the afternoon, not a full day. I sat with three of us on a desk, with as many as fifty or sixty lads in a class. We were sometimes educated by a member of the staff who was in his uniform and on leave. I went up to Penkhull Senior School and the headmaster was Mr Banks. He split the school into four houses – red, green, yellow and blue. You stayed in your house until you left school. We always started with scripture, followed by maths, English and then various other teachers took us for other subjects like history and geography. We had no woodwork, so what us lads had to do was cookery.

Albert Dale, born 1931

Tin School

I went to the nursery school, the tin school, on Leek Road. My most vivid memory of that is having to sleep in the afternoons which I hated. They actually made you lie on little truckle beds and put tape across your eyes if you didn't go to sleep; they forced you to go to sleep.

I just scraped through my 11 plus and I was sent to Chell High School and played truant there and was not exactly thrown out but was advised to go to another school, so I ended up at Caulden Road Secondary Modern. I never understood school; nobody ever explained why I was there so I never did anything very much and just scraped through. I don't know if you've heard of the Hornsea sit-ins, they affected the college where I was and we were invited to discuss any problems. The whole college met at the lecture theatre in the Longton part of the college. We discussed any problems that might arise and they were telling us how egalitarian the regime was in the art college but just that same year, the toilets that were shared amongst the staff and the students were closed to be used only by the staff. Toilets outside were to be used by the students. I used that point, questioning their claim to be egalitarian when they were creating a separation. Then the toilets were vandalised and I was suspected of it! It wasn't true.

Andrew Harrison, born 1947

Basics

I went to school at Brindley Ford, followed by Knypersley Hall Boys School. At Brindley Ford it was very basic. It was old desks, two at a desk, the old lift top desks with the inkwell. You had a wedge of wood with a nib at the end – that was the first writing implement I had. As you went up to the High School you bought your own fountain type of pen you know. There was no computers, no calculators. We had lessons which was mental arithmetic, which I don't believe they have any more, which learned you obviously to reckon your money up, accounts, all that, without having to use a piece of paper or calculator.

Charles Bibby, born 1955

Penkhull Council School, Stoke-on-Trent.

All Saints

I was a choirboy in All Saints' church which was a very high church. The vicar was known as Father even though it was Church of England. Once a year all of the local clergy would come to All Saints for a special service for the priesthood and we had to sing at it. We sang plain song which I didn't realise was quite unusual for a Church of England church. They did plain song with Latin responses and Greek responses.

Andrew Harrison, born 1947

New School

Matthew, our youngest, hadn't even been to school when we came up [to live in north Staffordshire in 1968]. So, we got him into Barlaston primary school, a pretty little school on the village green. Rebecca also went there – she was nine. She got on very well indeed. There was something exceptional going on with maths, a new idea about maths and she sailed through it. I'd been so worried about leaving London schools and needn't have worried.

Betty Smithers

Exams

When I think of Trentham Gardens I think of exams. I sat all of my exams for my degree course in the ballroom. For one of my exams I was positioned right at the back of the hall and in the moments when I could think of nothing to write I remember I just sat and stared at all the rows of students wondering what they were writing. In 1995 my graduation ceremony was also held in the ballroom. It was quite a sunny day so after the ceremony I went out in to the gardens to have my photograph taken with my parents. I remember trying to throw my cap up in the air and not being able to catch it.

Rachael Wagg, born 1973

Christmas

Christmas was always a special time. Dad collected a large Christmas tree from the market in Newcastle. It would be decorated with paper Chinese lanterns. Candles in small metal containers would be lit and always there would be a silver star on top of the tree. Christmas dinner was usually roast pork with all the trimmings, stuffing, apple sauce and carrots, sprouts and lovely gravy. We always had room for the delicious Christmas pudding which mum had made, and even room for a mince pie afterwards. Mum would then tell us a story. She was a very good storyteller. Just before Christmas 1925 money seemed to be in short supply. Maybe this was the forerunner of the depression years to come. Maurice and I were a little disappointed that there was not a 'Blackies Children's Annual' to greet us on Christmas morning. We always enjoyed sharing this annual, but mam and dad were able to buy it after Christmas at a sale price.

Eveline Shore, born 1919

Graduation

My graduation – class of 1999, one of the most memorable days of my life. The ceremony had the Lord Mayor as the Guest of Honour playing a fanfare down the main hall. When the ceremony was over all of the students threw their hats into the air. The reception after was amazing. There was a big marquee with chandeliers, a buffet, free drinks of champagne and a jazz band playing. It was a beautiful sunny day and

A school cookery class.

people were walking around the gardens to have their photographs taken. People were having picnics on the lawn.

Liz Dawson, born 1977

Liz Dawson's graduation at Trentham, 1999.

Playtime at Carmountside School, now demolished, in the 1950s.

CHAPTER 2
Leisure

On holiday in Southport, 1962.

Of the interviewees, a large number talked of trips out to the countryside where they walked or cycled. Some took this pastime particularly seriously, joining the scouts and going on camps. The countryside became very much a part of their lives and intrusions into this, including national service, were very much resented. Because many families were poor, they could not afford holidays; instead they took day trips or made the most of the wakes weeks. The annual Potter's Holidays saw many fairs and festivities in the streets and were the only times in which the air was clean as whole factories closed down and the kilns were allowed to cool, ready for maintenance. There was a sense of ease and contentment amongst the interviewees as they spoke of their trips to the cinema and their attempts to find a mate. As people's standard of living increased, families took their holidays in North Wales, Southport or Blackpool, often returning to the same boarding house each year. Before the car, the holidays were taken on the trains.

Ken Smith at Trentham.

Walks

Dad often used to take me for walks. On Sunday mornings we walked through Trent Vale, up through farmer Bill's meadow and Bobby's Lane. At the top of the lane was a farm where dad used to buy me a glass of fresh milk for a penny. Then we went on to Beech caves, coming back home over Jacob's Ladder into Trentham Park. If we were lucky we could see the deers grazing in the fern covered hills.

Eveline Shore, born 1919

Day Trips and Holidays

One of the outstanding memories of childhood was family Sunday's out. For most of the family, Sunday morning was a visit to the church and then home for Sunday lunch. Then the family, aunties, uncles, cousins and various other relatives used to assemble at my grandfather's house at Trentham known as the Old Post Office. It was quite a large house and once everyone was there we used to set off through Trentham Park, across on to fields up past the stream and lakes to Hanchurch. We had afternoon tea at Mrs Wright's farm which always consisted of boiled egg and bread and butter and a piece of slab cake which was fruit cake. The ladies and the children had one egg each, the men folk had two. It was always most enjoyable. We would then go into the woods and we'd got our own little spot in the woods with a rope swing fixed there.

Ken Smith, born 1929

Week's Holiday

Well as I say I was born in the Lymes, Hartshill and spent all of my childhood in Hanley, in Tintern Street off Wellington Road. Went to Wellington Road School eventually, the same one as Stanley Matthews. The family... typical working class family. Dad was a porcelain jollier, a skilled trade. Actually I do find that during the '30s when I was small, Dad's job was a lot better paid than others in the industry because we always had holidays. I mean I remember when I was a kid before the war, going to places like Torquay and Scarborough. You were lucky in those days if you got a week in Blackpool you know. It was a big thing if you had a week in Blackpool. I remember one of my friends went to Etruria for their holidays. Her aunty and uncle lived in Etruria so they went there for a week.

Graham Davies, born 1930

Backwater

Stoke seemed to be very much of a backwater because it was on a branch line of the railway and only one express train a day went to London, two maybe. And also the M6 hadn't been built. So Stoke seemed far away from everything and it was only when the railway was improved and the M6 opened up that the rest of the country seemed available. Our travel was school or Sunday school outings. The school would rent a train for the day and we'd go from Bucknall station, which no longer exists, on the mineral line. We'd go usually to New Brighton or Llandudno or Rhyl, no other places. They'd be day trips.

Andrew Harrison, born 1947

Day Trips

When we were children we had very few holidays, the odd day trip you know to

Holidaymakers in 1932 pose on a motorbike in a studio in Blackpool.

Trentham Hall was demolished in 1911/12. The grounds remained open to the people of Stoke.

Blackpool and places like that. There just wasn't the money to go on holiday. There was no going abroad. We once went to Scarborough for a week. That was the highlight of being a child. Obviously as I got older and started to earn money I went on holiday myself. I started to go to Europe, but even to this day I've never flown. Not because I'm afraid of it, I've just never seen the need to go round the Mediterranean. I'm happy to stay in this country.

Charles Bibby, born 1955

Wakes Week

Wakes Week... Well, you didn't go away so much then. When we were kids the Wakes used to be Pat Collins on the spare ground on Regent Road. Pat Collins was the proprietor I suppose of the fairground. It's Churchill House now. I just remember the noise from the steam organs, the rides and sideshows. When I was little before the war, we were taken down on just the one night when everybody took their kids. I remember walking back with a Mickey Mouse on a stick, his little legs moving. It broke before I got home. Towards the end they had a wall of death you paid sixpence to watch them belting round the inside of this sort of barrel. That was after the war.

Graham Davies, born 1930

Highlight

During the depression years of 1928 to the 1930s it was quite a highlight to travel by train to Alton Towers. Arriving at Alton railway station it was a short and pleasant walk to the entrance to the Towers. We would take with us sandwiches and home-made cake. It was a pleasure to walk through the lovely gardens and admire the arbour of trees.

High on one of the terraces we could sit and admire the beautiful scenery. Here we could listen to the Foden's Motor Work's band. The principal attraction was the playing of Harry Mortimer. He played the horn and the cornet to perfection. Even now, thinking back I can almost hear the strains of his music floating through the whole area of the Towers. We would buy a large jug of tea to enjoy with our sandwiches.

There was a very pleasant café among the trees called 'The Swiss Cottage' where afternoon teas could be bought. As Dad was out of work this was a luxury we could not afford. Walking up through the rock gardens, we could see high up on the skyline

A day trip to Alton Towers.

Children from Chell Secondary School are pictured at Stoke station on their way to Paris in 1956.

a large stone bust of the Earl of Shrewsbury, and written below it were the words 'He made the Desert smile'.

Dad would try to instil a little history in us about Prince Rupert, the 'Black Prince', who had way back visited the Towers. Our pleasures were simple in those days, and the sun always seemed to shine during our visits to the Towers.

When our children came along between 1945 and the 1950s, we used to take them to the Towers where they enjoyed boating on the lake and visiting the model and miniature railways. They could also climb the Flag Tower. This was all before the Towers became a theme park!

Eveline Shore, born 1919

Cycling to the Towers

I remember in the summer of 1970 a group of us, my brother, three friends and myself (then aged nine years old) decided on a day trip to 'the Towers'. Our only means of transport was by bicycle, and so we set out from Norton at about nine o'clock for the fifteen mile ride via Cheadle. My bike had one fixed gear; the others had bigger bikes with gears, so I had trouble keeping up. About a mile before Cheadle I remember hiding my then fashionable Harrington jacket in an oak tree with the others' jackets. It was a hot day and we had decided to shed some weight. After leaving our jackets and pullovers, we continued on to Alton and the 'fun house', our main objective!

There were no rides at Alton then, only the cable car and boat rides. The fun house had slides, rolling barrels and things like that. We parked our bikes near the main gate (inside) and they were still there when we returned after about two and a half hours.

The ride home was a little more sedate than going and we arrived home at about 6.30pm. Something I would not attempt today on a bicycle; traffic in 1970 was far less than today and not as fast!

Ian Shaw, born 1961

Pirate Ship

I remember visiting Alton Towers with my local youth group – I must have been about eleven years old. In particular I remember going on the Pirate Ship. I sat in between my older sister and her friend right at the back of the ship. They had to literally hold me down because as we swung backwards and forwards I was just lifting out of my seat. When the park was beginning to close down for the day we went on the Corkscrew for the last time. We actually ended up going on the ride about ten times. We just kept getting off and running round to go on it again because there were no queues. I remember finding the ride really scary at the time though these days it is quite tame compared to other rides.

Rachael Wagg, born 1973

The Gardens

I must have been about seven years of age when I paid my first of very many visits to Trentham Gardens. We would walk from

Alton Towers 2000. (Courtesy of Don McPhee and The Guardian)

Springfields along the road close to the gardens' entrance. There were some black and white cottages where one could buy afternoon teas. I was allowed free entrance to the gardens with my Rupert Badge from the *Daily Express*. We would take a pleasant walk through the beautiful, well laid out gardens, have a trip on one of the motor boats and paddle in the paddling pool. It was interesting to visit the stables and coach houses where the horses and carriages were housed in days gone by. There were some lovely buildings in good repair during those days. It was fascinating to obtain a bar of Fry's chocolate from the machine which was newly put up. One time I had my photograph taken for six pence. It was quite good but faded after a short while. I did not visit the gardens in my early teens when they started to have ballroom dances in the ballroom. My hobby was an outdoor life, mainly cycling. During the war years when I worked as a bus conductress, I took many, many double decker bus loads from Stoke to Trentham Gardens on Sundays. There was a special return fare at the price of six pence. After the war, we used to take our two young sons to Trentham Gardens. The younger one in a pram, the elder one on his tricycle. We would walk around the lake, enjoying the fresh country air. The children enjoyed playing in the soft grassy woodland. There was always some new attraction of nature to admire. We could feed the swans and listen to the sweet song of the many birds.

Eveline Shore, born 1919

Sunday Treat

I was born in 1944 and lived with my mother, brother, grandmother and grandfather in Lower Foundry Street, off Trinity Street in Hanley. Whilst my mother had to work, my grandmother stayed at home and looked after us. Her favourite pastime was to take us to Trentham Gardens. What a treat it was. The excitement would start on probably the Monday before the Sunday we were going to the gardens. She used to tell us if we were good all week she had a treat in store for us at the weekend; we always knew what it was! As the week wore on, we became more and more excited until Sunday morning; we could barely keep still.

After lunch, Grandma would pack a picnic and off we would go. The bus stop was just at the bottom of our street, on Trinity Street. For me, the day started there. If it was a double decker we would run upstairs and try to get the front seat. If it were a single decker we would always sit at the back. I loved to watch the clippie giving out the different colour tickets out of a wooden rack which was held over the shoulder. Later on, these were replaced with a little metal machine on which the amount of the fare was dialed and a ticket dispensed automatically. It took about half an hour to reach Trentham. It seemed like a lifetime to us. The bus stopped outside and my brother and I, followed by Grandmother, would walk happily into the gardens. I think there may have been a small charge to pay for entrance.

We always went the same way round. Past the ballroom on the left, in front of the lake to the bluebell woods. How I loved those woods! When the bluebells were out I thought it was heaven on earth. I always took a little straw basket with me so I could fill it with wild flowers, bluebells, buttercups, daisies and probably dandelions, to take back home to my mother. Sometimes, we would walk through the woods to the swimming pool and sometimes we would ride on the little train. We always walked one way and took the train the other way. I remember the swimming pool well although we were not allowed to go into the water. We would play happily round the edge and Grandmother would find someone to talk to whilst she watched us constantly so that we did not come to any harm. Grandmother would have a cup of tea and she would buy my brother and I a 'Rikki', which was a type of orange juice, and a packet of crisps.

After a while, we would pack up at the pool and maybe go to the lakeside where we would probably have our little picnic. Grandmother had quite bad feet so she could not walk too far all in one go so we sat down quite often, usually around the lakeside. There were pleasure craft on the lake and sometimes we would go for a trip round the lake.

At about five o'clock we were all so tired that we could hardly walk back to the entrance to catch the bus back home. But we all had a wonderful day and the memories stay with me even now.

Trentham Gardens was always crowded back then and the sun always seemed to shine. I don't remember it ever raining during our trips but I suppose it must have done on occasions as we went quite regularly. Things were different back in the 1940s and the 1950s. People did not have much money so to have a place like Trentham Gardens on their doorstep was wonderful and gave people an opportunity to get away from the dirt and grime of the pot banks and pits for a short time. It was like a different world to the back streets of Hanley and the rest of the Potteries.

Jean Wilson, born 1944

Swimming Pool

I also remember trips to Trentham Gardens. One day in 1968 or thereabouts, I went with my older sister to the swimming pool. It was the first open-air swimming pool I had ever seen. We took the bus to Trentham and then the light railway to the swimming pool inside the gardens. After an hour or so in the pool we went back towards the Hall on the railway and hired out a pedalo for a trip on the lake. Almost every visitor took a packed lunch and I remember hundreds of people sitting on the grass, eating sandwiches and drinking tea from a Thermos. Afterwards we boarded the 'Trentham Gardens Special', run by PMT, back to Hanley and then another bus back home to Norton.

Ian Shaw, born 1961

Summer

I can remember great memories of Trentham Gardens. The first thing that comes to mind was an event that happened every year in the summer. I was about thirteen and each summer the whole family would go to Trentham Gardens. There was so much going on you didn't know which way to turn. There were masses of flower beds and on the left was the huge lake. There were boats and jet skis racing up and down. My favourite though, was the animals. There were a few ponies that would stroll about the place and even rabbits to feed. Then we'd all go to the cafe and buy ice cream before going on the fun fair. It was brilliant. There were flashing arcade games, dodgems, waltzers, and it was like being at Blackpool and

Water skiing on Trentham Lake. (Courtesy of Don McPhee and The Guardian)

you got that buzzing feeling as if you were actually on holiday.

Clare Swetmore, born 1981

Camping

I went to Trentham Gardens camping when I was about eight. We went for the night in our trailer tent and took my cousin as his parents were going to a wedding. We had a great weekend; it was hot so we were able to ride on the open-air railway. There was a great adventure playground and marquees and shops. I think that we were able to take a boat out on the lake and visit a farm. At night we went into the hall itself. The next day my grandparents and auntie and uncle came and we all had a great time. We had our lunch outside and then went and explored the site further. I desperately wanted to go for the weekend again but the lake disappeared and apparently most of the attractions that they were starting to build went with it. When the lake returned some years later I made a return visit. I didn't enjoy it the same as I was too old and the lake had grown into a haven for water sports such as jet skis.

Lisa Jeffries, born 1973

Cubs

My cousin who was a little younger than me, he'd joined the cubs. I'd never thought about joining the cubs really but when I did reach eleven there was a fellow lived close by that was in the scouts and he took me along to the scouts in Hanley and I sort of stayed with the scouts then for fifty years. I saw various changes both in activities and uniform and actually this year there is a complete new change of uniform.

Occasionally we'd go to Kibblestone in those days but we were always known as isolationists our scout troop were because we'd got our own campsite at Tittensor and that's where we'd go most of the time because it was like a second home really, you know. The warden at Kibblestone used to call us isolationists because we didn't go to Kibblestone very often, mainly only for special camps like a visit by the chief scout or something like that. We were the 2nd Hanley YMCA. That had got a long history. It started in 1908 as two separate troops. One met in the kitchen of the scoutmaster at the time, the other met at an outbuilding at the Observatory Inn in Hanley. Then in 1910 the two groups combined and came under the umbrella of the YMCA. That was when we had to be officially registered in London and there was a scout troop at, I think it was Longport, that way somewhere. Their application was received just before ours, so they became the 1st Stoke-on-Trent; we were the 2nd Stoke-on-Trent although we were actually the first to start.

Ken Smith, born 1929

Co-op Youth Club

I used to go to the Co-op Youth Club. The room is still there I think. If you go down High Street in Tunstall, go along to Asda, well on the corner there is a door with some steps going up and it was up at the top, above the Co-op shops which were altogether there, the butchers and grocers and so on. Anybody could go and they used to have quizzes, dances, and I remember going on the Co-op conference for young people. There was a boy from Tunstall and myself who went as delegates to Yorkshire which was quite exciting you know. We were about sixteen and they had all sorts of lectures.

Brenda Bailey, born 1928

Youth Clubs

As a teenager I used to… I was very much into youth clubs. There was one youth club from my old school at Wellington Road. I think most of the schools had a youth club. I always went to what I consider to be the best one, in Shelton, and it was called the Rotary Youth Club. I believe it was originally started by the Rotary Club but when we went I don't think it had any associations with the Rotarians as such. I remember that every Friday we used to get the Young Communists outside trying to

A 'Greetings from the Potteries' postcard, sold to raise funds for the Scouts.

convert us into communism. We weren't political at all you know! But it was a damn good club that one was with a very good drama group. We always seemed to come away with the best adjudication. And then it folded up and it wasn't until the late 50s that they said anyone over twenty-one could do it. The leader, Richard Pipe, got in touch with a lot of the old drama group and asked them if they would like to do it again and we did an excerpt from *Blythe Spirit* in the Mitchell and got a super adjudication. They had a good table tennis thing, I was no good at table tennis mind you. Good discussion groups and a music society and we'd go on little music trips to orchestral concerts.

Graham Davies, born 1930

The Festival of Britain

Socially speaking we found the Festival of Britain immensely exciting and enjoyable. We used to arrange with a next door neighbour to mind our two children, two small boys. After nine o'clock you could get in for a shilling. We walked from where we lived in West Hampstead, caught a tube straight through to Waterloo, got in one minute after nine o'clock and then we could spend a couple of hours drinking coffee, having snacks. If the weather was good, we were doing quicksteps and slow foxtrots, slow waltzes and all the rest of it in the beautiful concourse area between the Transport Pavilion and the Dome of Discovery. Set in the paving stones of the concourse were lights, the trees had

Brownhills High School perform The Countess Cathleen *in April 1943.*

lights around them. This was our first experience of this kind of approach to exterior designing. It was magic. Whenever we hear of people who write articles critical of the Festival of Britain, critical of it being a failed promotion, we are so surprised and feel so at odd with these views. They are invariably expressed by people who had no experience of it. It was all part of our experience of what life might become more like in the future.

Alick Smithers, born 1926

That's Entertainment

My brother and I, we used to go selling 'Sentinels' on a Saturday night, taking 'Sentinels' out. My sister would be courting I suppose and my mother would be working at an uncle's public house in Tunstall. My brother and I used to have a penny discount for selling the 'Sentinels' and on the Saturday night we used to spend ha'penny and we used to have a comic of about twenty pages. Then we used to take a great big dish to the chip shop for a ha'penny worth of chips and we used to put it on the front of the hearth and we'd have all these comics around us. And we always had a dog and the dog always was having pups. We used to bring the dog in and all the pups and all of us would eat out of this bowl. That was our Saturday night's luxury.

Elizabeth Stringer, born 1904

Wireless

It was in 1925 when I was almost six that we acquired our first crystal set. It was a Saturday and my dad had to work during the morning. We needed a pole to fix an aerial wire, so my mum, me and my brother were to collect one. We walked from our village at Springfield up to Newcastle-under-Lyme, a distance of about two miles and collected our pole which cost us five pence. We proudly walked home, my mother holding the front, my brother the back and me giving a bit of support in the middle. In the afternoon my dad dug a hole for the pole and secured it in place with stones. My Uncle Frank attached the aerial wire to the chimney pot. On the roof was my rag doll which one of my brother's pals had thrown up there a few months earlier. Uncle Frank threw it down but it fell to bits, strewing sawdust all around. I stared in disbelief and shouted at my brother. To pacify me, I was given a promise that I would be the first to listen to the wireless when it was fixed. Through the headphones I heard a lot of queer noises at first, then the miraculous sound of music as Uncle Frank fiddled with the cat's whisker. On Saturday mornings a gentleman called Philip Thornton told tales of his travels and this was one of my favourite programmes. We also listened to Children's Hour when we came home from school. My favourite character was a dragon called Grizzle. One night my mam told my brother Maurice that he could stay up and listen to an orchestral concert and when I found out I didn't want to be left out. But there were only two sets of headphones. Mother had a bright idea. She took a pretty green gas lampshade, turned it upside down and placed the two sets of headphones inside. Sitting close we could all hear the concert by Sir Hamilton Harty.

Eveline Shore, born 1919

Magic Lantern Shows

I remember the old magic lantern shows they used to have. It started with Frankie Reilly and my Uncle Arthur who had the newsagents in Pitts Hill. They used to do magic lantern shows in the church halls. They were mainly religious things, temperance and all this sort of thing but they were good evenings you know. They were very popular in the early days. You had lots of kids in there, sitting on benches and things.

Syd Bailey, born 1922

Cinema

Cinemas were closed for some time [at the outbreak of war] because they said if a bomb fell on a crowd in a cinema it would kill too many people. But they realised that the people were getting frustrated and, with not having enough food, being kept awake every night with the bombs falling, that they had to give them some recreation. So the cinemas opened again.

Angela Mellor, born 1915

Saturday Morning Shows

I was never a member of a minor's club but I used to go regularly to the Saturday morning shows. Originally we went to the Roxy in Glass Street, which was the low end of the market, that was two pence, then it was three pence for the Odeon and the Regent, but you could go upstairs for sixpence or something. They were the same films but a different ambience to the Roxy especially if you went to the Roxy on a Thursday night –you were drowned out by the Salvation Army next door. The Citadel had band practice on a Thursday evenings. Generally speaking the cinema was the only form of entertainment. I always went once a week and on one occasion I went four times, but that was a bit excessive!

Graham Davies, born 1930

Zulu

We used to go to the cinema in Biddulph and also Barber's Picture Palace in Tunstall which was along the Boulevard. I didn't belong to the matinee clubs or anything like that. When it first came out I liked the film *Zulu*. My grandfather took me. It was just a really good film. I enjoyed it and my grandfather had treated us, like.

Charles Bibby, born 1955

The Coliseum, Hope Street, Hanley.

Drama

I was very interested in drama groups. While I was at Sneyd Green, the person living next door to where I was living in digs, was engaged to one of the members of the New Era Players at Birches Head. So I got involved with them, joined them. They were one of the leading amateur drama groups in the area at that time. They performed in the church hall at Birches Head. That was quite a thing in itself. You had to erect the stage and all the scenery on the Sunday ready for the start on the Monday. You had a week's run and it finished on the Saturday. So on the Sunday you had to go and take all this stuff down. The first play we did was 'The Good Young Man' which was a comedy but I was also in various other things. Later on when I did things with them they did things like 'The Power and the Glory' which we did at the Old Vic. We did that in the round. We also did 'Our Town' also at the Old Vic.

Syd Bailey, born 1922

Cost of Living

In a sense, we had become ghettoised in Stoke-on-Trent. We had adjusted ourselves to a much lower cost of living here and although we had one or two opportunities to move back to London, financially and with four children to raise it would have been very difficult to do so. The difference between the cost of housing and accommodation in London compared with here was during that period... the gap was opening up considerably. It would have been extremely difficult. So I thought I'd better look for a job in which I'd be happier and fortunately found one very quickly at Doulton.

When we moved up to north Staffordshire of course our contact with Stoke was relatively limited. We lived either at Barlaston or at Stone and if we wanted to shop or whatever we tended to go to Stafford. I had been up in Stoke visiting various of the Wedgwood factories there and I took Betty up once or twice. Without being very self-conscious about it we tended to orientate our experiences for shopping and leisure elsewhere. Funnily enough one of the few things that really swayed us to the idea of coming up to north Staffordshire had been my experiences of the old Victoria Theatre when it had been in Victoria Road between Stoke and Newcastle. For all that we were able when we were in London to go to West End theatre, to Covent Garden for opera, we could go to music hall which was still quite lively in Edgeware Road and places like that. So there were quite a lot of popular forms of entertainment but I had not come across theatre in London at that time that was better than what Peter Cheeseman was doing here in Stoke at the old Victoria Theatre. We loved the idea of theatre in the round. Plus also the Potteries was still a place that accommodated the factories of such famous names and we had relatives and friends who would come and stay with us and they all knew of Stoke-on-Trent because of the names of Doulton, Wedgwood, Minton, Spode and so on. We felt some degree of pride in Stoke for all that we found it a city which was still very untidy. There was never a feeling from our friends and relatives of 'what are you doing living in Stoke-on-Trent?' The place wasn't significantly different from any other in the country. It wasn't particularly cut off. The

M1 still had to get up to Leeds, the M6 was still being built through from Birmingham. The train services were improving and intercity services were speeding up.

Alick Smithers, born 1926

Disco

I remember going to the very first disco that was held in the swimming pool at Trentham Gardens in 1966. I was nineteen years old and wore a pink gingham bikini – my first ever bikini. It was a really hot Friday night and I remember dancing and swimming to music from The Beatles, The Searchers and in particular The Animals 'House of the Risin' Sun'.

Sue Wagg, born 1947

Music

I was quite an eccentric type and my interests were more jazz and folk music. The '60s were the time of the folk song revival and there was a very lively club at the Red Lion in Stoke. The Red Lion has since disappeared completely; it was by the churchyard near to the D-road roundabout. We used to sing there and heard some of the most famous singers of the day, Ewan MacColl, Peggy Seeger, Martin Carthy who went on to sing in Steeleye Span and the Watersons, Dave Swarbrick who was the violinist for Fairport Convention was there, Bert Jansch sang there, Luke Kelly. Stoke was quite lively but it wasn't a centre for the folk revival I don't think.

Andrew Harrison, born 1947

Television

The lady next door, Mrs Comberbach, was the first to have a television. She had a nine inch television. Thinking back on it, she must have been a very generous lady. She was very likeable. She had all the kids from Garner Street in to look at this nine inch box. They were sitting on the sideboard, on the cupboards. They were all over the sitting room. And she used to sit with a little dog called Suki, and she'd let us stay as long as we wanted. Her husband was an old man, Bill, who sat up the corner and occasionally used to spit in the grate.

Rhona Atkins, born 1938

Vidor Radio

The only thing I can recollect which we used to have for entertainment at night was the Vidor radio. It used to have an accumulator which you used to have to take to the shop for charging it up. I can always remember my father when he used to say 'I think the battery might be running low. Wet your fingers, put that on the positive, that on the negative,' and of course when you flew off your chair you knew the battery was charged up! He was a bit of a comedian the old chap was. But I remember one day one of my brothers turned the radio on and he couldn't quite get a station so we started fiddling at the back and a puff o' smoke came out. So we stood in the room wondering what the old chap would say. One of us ran along to the end of the entry and we waited for him to come up Keelings Road. If he was walking straight you knew you were all right, but if he was swaying a bit we used to run upstairs and go and hide under the beds. When he came in the first thing he did was switch the radio on and of course nothing came out. We heard this big booming voice and we were shaking like leaves under the bed. We all blamed each other and of course we all got a bloody good thrashing because we'd put pay to the radio which was the entertainment. We used to listen to 'The Man in Black', 'The Wilfred Pickles Show' and Violet Carson on the piano. Shows like that.

Roy Furnival, born 1936

And the band played on...

Trentham Gardens... How did I know that that day in 1963 would lead to one of the most exciting periods of my life?

The Swinging Sixties was a good time to be a teenager. Most young people had money in their pockets, beautiful clothes to wear and new exciting music to listen to. Elvis had come onto the scene in the 1950s, had done his national service, mainly in Germany, returned to the States and had taken up his career again. But over here in England, new groups were coming onto the scene, mainly from the Liverpool area. The most popular group in England at that time were four young men with the peculiar name of The Beatles. One of their records, 'Please, Please Me', was released on 27 March 1963 and overnight became a smash hit. From then on, everywhere The Beatles played was pandemonium.

Back to 1963, October I think, The Beatles were booked to appear at the ballroom inside Trentham Gardens. My friend and I did not have tickets for the show but went along anyway. At that period in our lives we wrote songs – or so we told ourselves!

Looking back now they were a collection of verses to which music could have been put if somebody had the ability to do so. My friend and I certainly did not have that ability! When we arrived at Trentham Gardens the atmosphere was tremendous. We walked around for some time and then decided to go round the back of the ballroom, not really knowing what we were looking for. It was dark by now. As we were pushing our way through the undergrowth, immediately in front of us stood a very tall man looking down at us. I do not know who was the most surprised. He asked us what we were doing. We told him that we wrote songs and we thought The Beatles might be interested in them. Looking back now I cannot even believe we said that. Anyway, I don't know if it was our lucky day, but he told us he was one of The Beatles road managers, Malcolm Evans, and although we could not see The Beatles then as they were preparing for the show, if we liked we could go along to the North Stafford Hotel, opposite Stoke Railway Station, the following day and we could spend some time with the boys. He was such a gentleman. Not rough as you would expect a road manager to be. A gentle giant really. We were on cloud number nine!

Next day, at the appointed time, we turned up at the North Stafford Hotel and Mal (as we came to know him) came to meet us and took us up to the room to meet The Beatles. The press were there at the time and they took some pictures of my friend and I with The Beatles. They looked at some of our songs. If I remember correctly, they were quite complimentary. After a while it was time to go and we thought that would be the end of everything. Mal came to the entrance of the hotel with us and even thanked us for coming. He then said if we wished to see The Beatles on stage at any time, all we had to do was turn up at the stage door and ask for him and he would come for us. At that time we really thought he was just saying that to be kind. But not so. A short while afterwards The Beatles were appearing quite close and we decided to go and see what would happen. We did exactly as Mal said, pushed our way through the crowds at the stage door, knocked on it and when the doorkeeper came, told him who we were and that we would like to see Malcolm Evans. Within minutes, he arrived and took us inside. He took us into the dressing room where The Beatles were just finishing getting ready for the show that night. We talked to all of them and Mal insisted that we watched the show from the wings at the side of the stage. It was fantastic! The same thing happened a few times and then George Harrison told us that we could telephone his mother should we wish to get in touch with Mal for any reason. I spoke to George's mother quite a few times on the phone and she was very nice. We also visited Malcolm's home when we were in Liverpool for a show, as he wanted us to meet his wife. She was a very nice person too and made us very welcome. I remember that night we missed our train home from Liverpool and I think we had to wait for a mail train or something similar. We got home at about four o'clock in the morning.

I remember on one occasion talking to Paul McCartney and he was telling me about their visit to America during which they had been invited by Elvis to go along to his house. Paul told me that they were so star struck that all they could do was stare at Elvis. Elvis got tired of that after a while and said that if they did not want to talk to him, he was going to go to his bedroom. It was not that they did not want to talk to him, they just did not know what to say. Anyway, that seemed to break the ice and they got on famously after that and finished up jamming together. Now that would have been really something, had a home record been made that night – The Beatles and Elvis together. What a smash hit that would have been!

Our visits with Malcolm Evans and The Beatles probably went on for about eighteen months or so until I moved to the north east of England to work for Imperial Chemical Industries. We did correspond for a while but The Beatles were spending more and more time in America and on world tours and eventually the letters stopped.

That was a wonderful and exciting part of my life for which I thank Mal and The Beatles for making it so, and it was a time I shall never forget. The ending is quite sad though. In or around 1990 I was driving to work and there was a news item on the radio. It said that Malcolm Evans, road manager to The Beatles had been shot dead in hotel rooms by police in Los Angeles. No further comment was made and I have never been able to find out the full circumstances surrounding his death. Whatever happened, all I can say is that he was a very fine young man and a very kind man and he made some of my teenage years very happy. But if I had not gone to Trentham Gardens that night…

Jean Wilson, born 1944

The Beatles

Another memory I have is of going to see The Beatles perform in the ballroom at Trentham Gardens. It was either 1964 or 1965. Everyone was screaming and it was so crowded that people were stacking tables on top of one another and climbing on them in order to have a better view.

Sue Wagg, born 1947

Pulp

My second great memory of Trentham Gardens is from 25 November 1998. My favourite band, Pulp, were doing a live concert. We got there about an hour early, waiting for the entrance doors to open. When they did, me and my friends raced to the stage before buying our Pulp t-shirts. When Pulp did come on stage the atmosphere was buzzing and as soon as the music started everybody was jumping up and down. Then later on Jarvis Cocker asked us if there was any famous people from the Potteries. Everyone shouted out 'Robbie Williams' and he just grinned and rolled his eyes back which I thought was quite funny. That night was brilliant and it was the ideal venue for a band like Pulp to do a live concert.

Clare Swetmore, born 1981

Dancing

Alick loves classical music and I love jazz like crazy. We love dancing but not jigging about, proper dancing. We love slow foxtrots and tangos and things like that. I can't stand sequence dancing when everyone does the same thing. I want it to be free. When the Longton Town Hall was opened we used to go every Monday afternoon. I used to rush home from college at lunch time, we rushed up there. It was only records but it was wonderful. How many years ago was that? Six, ten years ago? It was proper ballroom dancing and it was great! We didn't go to Trentham except two or three times. We've been at the invite of friends and to the Mayor's Ball once or twice.

I'm very pleased about the Cultural Quarter and I love the museum. I can't remember when I first visited but I used to bring my students here. Jean Muir came once too, in 1982. It was the day we moved. I went into college that day and took with me some clothes to change into and brought some students to see Jean Muir and her exhibition. Coming into the museum these last few years has been marvellous. I love the improvements to the Victoria Hall. We've been to more concerts at the Victoria Hall these last few years since it reopened than we had

The Regent Theatre, recently reopened in the centre of the Cultural Quarter.

in the whole of our previous time in north Staffordshire. The quality of the experience of going to the Victoria Hall and the Regent Theatre is immeasurable. If things continue to improve like this then there is a future for Stoke. But I think people generally resist change. They like things to be the same as they always were. We're talking conservative with a small 'c' quite honestly. I like to live with the now and the future. I love history but you have to move on and make things comfortable for yourself and pleasurable.

Betty Smithers

Ceramica

I'm very sad that Ceramica has run into the difficulties it now faces. People should hold back from making judgements about Ceramica based solely on its appearance and until it is completed. It's frustrating that because of the financial difficulties work has stopped and has stopped for far too long. I just want to see it finished. Once it is achieved then I think there will be a big jump forward for urban improvement in Burslem.

Alick Smithers, born 1926

The Monkey Run

I was allowed ten shillings up until the week before I got married. Ten shillings a week! But out of that I had to pay my bus fare to and from work, either that or walk. If I wanted anything to eat at work it had to come out of that ten shillings. Also my bus fare to go courting in Hanley at night. So there was very little left of my ten shillings.

Rhona Atkins, born 1938

Piccadilly, Hanley, c. 1948.

Town Hall Square, Longton in 1951 – notice the milk bar.

Cafés

The monkey run that I remember was originally Piccadilly and then it became Hope Street. I didn't use the monkey run as a monkey run to be honest, we used to go and see people we knew actually, not for a casual pick up. I'm just talking for myself. There used to be a cafe, Leena's, half way down and we used to go in there for a cup of tea. There weren't many places you could get a cup of tea in Hanley. The only other one I remember was one that was opposite the post office, the main post office, the general, and it was called Kay's Dive-in Café and there used to be a sign of a diver diving down. They were open to possibly midnight and you could only ever get a cup of tea, seldom they would have a cake you know. I only ever used it very late at nights if you were wandering around. It was more a place for down and outs from what I remember. Leena's in Hope Street, a lot of the young people got into Leena's. I'm afraid the other ones, the milk bars were just before my time.

Graham Davies, born 1930

Courting

I don't think I really knew myself what courting was all about. I mean, you used to go out and pick girls up, but we were so naive it was absolutely ludicrous to think about it today. I mean, if you kissed a girl and you gave her a cuddle and then went home, you probably thought she was pregnant. This is true! We were very naive. In the '40s and '50s if you saw a girl's ankle, you know, that was something. Girls at the age of fifteen or sixteen looked like young children compared to the girls of today. It was just a matter of going out. You see,

Lamb Street, Hanley.

Tower Square, Tunstall, once part of the monkey run.

when you're young you think you own the world. You've started work, started in the pit. You go round Hanley and pick a few women up. Same as the younger generation do today, except they've got more to do. They've got cars and motor bikes, plenty of money and nice clothes. I think if I had mentioned I was going out with somebody my father would have gone up the wall. He'd have been thinking 'Roy's got a girl. I wonder if he's leaving home? That's another breadwinner who's left home.' As far as you were concerned you were going out with your mates. You was either in the pictures or you were going up Hanley or something.

The monkey run used to start in Hanley Market Square. I remember there used to be a place there that sold coffee and a cup of tea or Oxo. Everyone used to hang around Sherwin's corner and we'd sort of club together, a gang of lads and a gang of girls and off you'd go. You'd go down Lamb Street and into Stafford Street, down to Hope Street. At the bottom there was a café where in actual fact Arnold Bennett was born. You'd drink tea or coffee and they had a jukebox in there. You'd just swan around looking for the girls like and when you picked one up you didn't know what the bloody hell to do with them. You'd walk back up to the square with them and you'd probably give them a peck and a good night. You'd thought you'd had a wonderful night.

Roy Furnival, born 1936

Getting Together

Tunstall High Street and the park used to be a monkey run as they called it. It was just young men and young women sort of eyeing each other up and catching them up. It wasn't in a rowdy, noisy sort of way; no hankey pankey in public! It was just a happy time. Lots of folks got to know each other. It mostly took place on Sundays.

Brenda Bailey, born 1928

Sunday Nights

I knew there was fellas out there and I fancied one or two of them. But the big problem was how to get round my mother to get out there and get at them. I used to wait for Sunday nights and casually ask my mum if I could go to the Palace in Hanley. It wasn't so much as the Palace I was interested in as the monkey run afterwards. It had to be a quick up and down Hope Street because I didn't want my mother to know that I'd been down Hope Street. I used to tell my mum that they'd put an extra picture on that took up an hour of my time.

Rhona Atkins, born 1936

An Active Life

Then someone hit on the idea of being a bit more mobile and most of the youngsters had got cycles so the parents set out to get cycles and in a lot of cases they had tandems. The youngest married couple I remember had got a young baby not to be left out, so they had a side car fitted to their tandem. One favourite route we used to go on was out through Stone towards Rugeley and turn off to Milford Common. Then we'd have a picnic on Milford Common. There was always a van there selling tea. Very popular Milford Common was. There was them who had got cars, but very few had in those days.

It was a popular place for cyclists and you could have a walk onto Cannock Chase. We'd make our way back to Trentham via Stafford and usually call in a pub on the way. The ladies and children would sit outside while the men folk went in for a drink you know. It was very rare for the women to go in the pub, mainly because they wanted to keep their eyes on the children.

Ken Smith, born 1929

Trips

While I was at college I'd been interested in the mountaineering club and one of my mates had taken me up to Snowdonia. We stayed at the youth hostel. So while I was teaching at Bradeley I started taking groups in the holidays up to North Wales. In about 1955 I moved schools to Chell and we extended it then, started going abroad. I took a party to Paris. There were one or two commercial firms that were beginning to specialise in school parties and I went to Paris with one of them, but there weren't an awful lot of them. They were only just beginning. Having done that I decided then that I could save money for the kids by arranging them myself. I was interested in Switzerland; I had one or two connections with people in Switzerland. So I arranged a trip there. It was fantastic. The first one I arranged was a summer trip. I went by train from here to London, spent a night at the Earl's Court Youth Hostel in London, then travelled by train down to the coast and across the Channel. Took a train down to Bern. Had breakfast there and went on to Thun. Went on the lake to Interlaken, taking a train to Wilderswille. Stayed the night in the youth hostel there. From there went up to Wengen by train and stayed in the youth hostel there. Then I took them up the Jungfrau, back down to Grindelwald and

Chell Secondary School children on holiday in Switzerland in 1955.

Sir Harold Clowes, Lord Mayor, with Dr Bircher, First Secretary to the Swiss Embassy, at Chell School in 1958.

stayed in the youth hostel there. Hiked up the Jock pass down into Engleberg in the next valley. Then we went to Lucerne and caught a train back. The whole thing only cost about £30 per child. When we came back we had meetings for the parents. We invited them and showed them slides and films. Near the end of the time at Chell in the late '50s, when we invited the Lord Mayor, Alderman Harold Clowes, his daughter who was Lady Mayoress, the kids dressed up in Swiss costume and sang Swiss songs. We had the First Secretary from the Swiss Embassy in London come up. We even went and bought Swiss pastries from a shop up in Alderley Edge. It was quite a thing.

Syd Bailey, born 1922

Exercise

I don't run anymore, I used to cycle a lot. I was keen on that but rowing, or sculling as you might call it, has always been my hobby. It's my great love. I think it's the most desirable form of exercise. You're exercising every part of your body, arms, legs, stomach muscles everything and you're in the open and you're battling against the weather.

Sam Singer, born 1911

Speedway

There was the speedway up Sun Street. The main thing about the speedway was the excitement of it all, the noise of the engines revving up, the smell of oil. And it was a thing to see all the cinders flying. As the bikes went round the cinders flew and people standing on the corners would get covered in these things. There was some old pit mounds overlooking Sun Street and people could watch the speedway from up there, without paying or getting into the stadium at all. But they hadn't got the excitement down there of it. The Potters weren't like in the premier league, more like the first division and the races were usually on a Saturday night; they used to get good crowds down there.

Syd Bailey, born 1922

Badminton

Badminton was very popular in this area. We had a team at our church at Westley Place in Tunstall. It used to meet twice a week and then we had matches with other churches and clubs. In Norton, Kidsgrove, Chell and Ball Green, there'd be badminton teams. At Wesley Place my mother was in charge of the refreshments. They used to have a strange mixture which people thought was beautiful, jam and cheese sandwiches – together! I couldn't eat it!

Brenda Bailey, born 1928

Water Polo

Another thing that was very popular in Tunstall was water polo in Tunstall baths. Feelings used to run very high at matches there. Almost riots at times. There was always a banner across the baths advertising the matches at eight o'clock on a Wednesday. Malcolm Upright was about six foot seven and they were always accusing

Artist's impression of the dance hall at Trentham Gardens before completion.

Naylor's, Barber's and Pemperton's dance at the Floral Hall, Tunstall Park, 1952.

him of standing on the bottom! They had a very successful team.

Syd Bailey, born 1922

The Essoldo

Originally it [the Essoldo] was a roller skating place, yes, but that was before my time. I remember my mother's friend, I always used to call her aunty, went roller skating and she had her hair in plaits that stuck out as though the wind was blowing them. Previous to that it was a huge factory called Dimmock's I think, a massive place.

Graham Davies, born 1930

Socials

There was a lot of dances, that sort of thing. Trentham was going full blast. There were dances every Saturday night at the town halls. Later on I got involved because my father-in-law helped to run some of these dances. I used to go and help him out on Saturdays, taking money, stewarding and so on. The Floral Hall in Tunstall Park was used a lot for dances and parties and social events.

Syd Bailey, born 1922

Archery

My grandfather, if he wasn't looking after the gardening, looked after the archery. It was a big thrill for us to help him collecting the arrows.

There must have been eight targets all set up in a row in a fenced off area for safety in the late 1930s. [Years later in the Scouts] one fellow in the troop, Roy Hancock, known as Hank, was a great hunter. He'd got his own bow and arrows that he'd made. We'd seen him shoot rabbits with it and that used to supplement the meat rations at camp... Whenever we went to Trentham Hank would always go to the archery. He was that good he just had to pay for his first six arrows – if you won then you got another six free. He'd be on there for ages because he kept winning. It got to the point after a while when they'd say 'that's enough'.

Ken Smith, born 1929

June Jones, right, at her first ball, Trentham Gardens, 1957.

Cars

I passed my driving test in 1978. Up to now I've no convictions touch wood. I had a number of second hand cars and then in the early '80s I bought a Lada estate which was a new car. I then had two Fiestas which were new and at present I have a Renault Clio which I've also had from new. I use driving basically as a means of pleasure, getting out in the countryside. I enjoy walking, that sort of thing. It gets you out of the immediate area and into new areas rather than walking the same old trails all the time. Just flit up to a different area, park up and go for a walk.

Charles Bibby, born 1955

Learning to Drive

One Sunday I thought it would be a good idea if I learnt how to drive. So Albert let me drive up and down the lane a time or two and occasionally along the country road at the bottom of the lane which led to a place called Stableford. One Sunday I was driving the car down the lane but when we got to the bottom of the lane there were two policemen leaning over the fence talking. I should have gone on I suppose, but I panicked and Albert said 'Well let's pretend the car's stalled and I will take over.' Aren't we naive when we are young? The two policemen came over and asked to see my licence which of course I did not have. Out came the notebook and notes were made: no licence, no insurance, Albert aiding and abetting and so on. Were we scared? At the courts we waited nervously for our case to come up. The judge was a man called Mr Goodwin. He told us we were young and foolish and fined us four shillings with sixpence costs.

Eveline Shore, born 1919

North Staffs Federation

The North Staffs Federation has thirty-four clubs and it runs out in the region of approximately one thousand members. It covers a radius of sixteen miles of Stoke Church and your loft has to be within that radius to be a member. We have twenty races each year. We send approximately eight thousand birds on land racing. Pigeon racing is a great hobby when you get into it. There's a lot of enjoyment in it. It's the same as a fisherman enjoys his fishing. It's the relaxation as well. Especially as some of the time you can sit with your birds and watch them. Its observation which makes the difference between winning and losing really. The more time you spend with them and observe them, the better you become. Good pigeons always turn up again if they get half the chance. A good pigeon can be worth thousands.

Ted Smith, born 1928

Harry Brown's pigeon. (Courtesy of Stephen Wood)

School Sports

I used to enjoy sports at school, did all the athletics with them. We had our schools competitions, at Northwood stadium normally. I used to like sprinting, running but as I got older I started liking football and that was my main sport. I only actually played for my school twice and that was at the end of my final year. I played for Newcastle in every position except goal. In the works team I had a mate who lived up the road from me and played in goal. But he was nearly always late, so for the first ten minutes I'd play in goal. So I've played in every position. I've had trials with a small team called Liverpool, Nottingham Forest when Brian Clough was there and the local team Port Vale but I couldn't get to Liverpool and Nottingham because me brother started work and was the one with the transport and used to take me. That's when I got the trials with Port Vale.

Kevin Webster, born 1958

Car Rally

I also remember going to watch a car rally at Trentham Gardens. During the day there were lots of people watching and then it started to get cold and dark and most people left. We stayed until the very end of the rally and we were glad that we did as there was a surprise fireworks and laser show. This was set to music and was brilliant as it took place over the lake. We had an excellent view because everyone else had gone and there was only a handful of us left.

Rachael Wagg, born 1973

Football

I'm the only girl in our family and all my cousins are like lads and with my brother they used to get me outside to play football with them. So you just do. I'd have some friends who'd come up; they were lads as well. We'd all play football every night. I think it just grows on you. You'd be playing on a field and other kids would join in.

Clare Swetmore, born 1981

Park Life

The park used to be very busy and you always met the same people there. We had 'Our Gang' – in a nice sense! I got to know people who didn't go to my school because we used to meet and play in the park. Alex Humphries used to come into the park and was one of our gang there because he was friendly with a boy called John Downing who's father was the police inspector in Tunstall. We just used to play games and have fun really. I think when television came in we started to stop going in the park. Also our age, as you got older you stopped doing that sort of thing.

Brenda Bailey, born 1928

City Parks

Stoke-on-Trent does have a wonderful legacy of its industrial past, and that is the city parks. Beautiful green lungs, sometimes neglected too much but complemented by the extensive green space industrial reclamation areas. It is a surprisingly green city if you look carefully, and it is surrounded by a wonderfully varied and beautiful rural hinterland which is very easily

Park gates, Tunstall.

Rose garden, Burslem Park.

reached. When I came to live here I found myself thinking that here is a place where a pound is a pound, not some devalued coinage. People work hard for modest reward and value what they have. In a real sense I felt I was going back in time a bit. To be here felt something like my working class childhood in South London, a place where an older fashioned but enduring social ethic is lived daily. An ethic of self-sufficiency, good humour and local pride. Maybe that's why I feel at home here, despite the long passage of the years since then.

Roger Brown, born 1945

Floral Hall

The Floral Hall had a long oblong hall with double doors leading into the conservatory. The conservatory was really a showpiece. It was really beautiful and people used to come specially to Tunstall, to go into the park and go into the conservatory. There was a little fountain in it and a little pool. It had very exotic plants and was beautifully kept. I can't remember there being anything like it in any of the other parks. The hall was used mainly for people to hire for functions. There was a little shop on one corner which opened for ice creams and sweets and things like that. We had our silver wedding party there. It had good kitchens, a bar and plenty of space for parking. It closed a long time ago now needing a lot of work doing on it and the council hadn't got the money. I think a local committee has raised money to renovate what's left. I think it's got a new roof on it. But the conservatory has gone altogether. I think one reason they have had all the vandalism in the park is because there isn't a parkie now, an attendant. We used to be really scared of them and they did used to chase us with a stick.

Brenda Bailey, born 1928

Ravensdale FC, 1920.

Carnival

For several years they had a carnival in Tunstall. It was run by the local Labour Party for charity. My father-in-law was the treasurer of the local Labour Party so he roped me in on that. One year I remember the main attraction, the main person, was the Carnival Queen of Great Britain. She brought all her uncles and cousins and they all turned up at our house for tea.

Syd Bailey, born 1922

Football Crazy

When we used to play football we never had shin pads. We used to stick newspapers down us socks. And we played in pumps or clogs or Wellington boots.

Roy Furnival, born 1936

Football Loyalty

I used to go to football a fair bit in those days, Stoke most of the time because I'd been involved with Stoke even from Oswestry where I used to live. I used to come over from there with family for matches. In fact a young lad played for Stoke, who came from Oswestry, and my father actually came with him when he transferred to Stoke. Later on when Vale were having their long run, I got quite interested in the Vale and used to go and watch them.

Syd Bailey, born 1922

Football Matches

They must have been very forward thinking in Stoke and did a lot for the ordinary people because my father was in the local football team, Ravensdale, and thousands of people must have watched them. You'd get two or three thousand people turning up to watch a match. There was great rivalry with the Goldenhill Wanderers you know. The churches very often had teams and they were in leagues. They also had cricket teams as well.

Brenda Bailey, born 1928

Referee

I ran the line in the FA Cup final between Liverpool and Sunderland. I've visited Wembley five times. The Cup Final in 1992. In '93 I went there twice, no three times, once for the semi-final of the FA Cup, the Coca-Cola Cup Final that year between Arsenal and Sheffield Wednesday and one of the football league play-offs. I once refereed a local Sunday Cup game in which I allowed a dog to score a goal. It's a good job it happened to me because I have got a sense of humour and I've had to live with it since 1987! A few years ago a magazine called '4-4-2' did an article called 'The Ten Worst Refereeing Decisions of All Time' and my decision was in there at number six. My excuse is that when the dog scored the goal, I was badly positioned and didn't actually see the dog! It didn't stop me moving up the ladder though. It's nice that these things happen.

John Holditch, born ????

Great Goals

My favourite Stoke player is Mark Stein aka 'The Golden One' who scored great goals at great times, especially Wembley '92. The best manager was Lou Macari. We won the Division Two Championship and the Auto Glass Trophy at Wembley and we

Wesley Place Cricket Club, 1920.

looked like a football team that knew what they were doing which we haven't done since he left.

Richard Rogers, born 1969

City of Stoke Ladies

I've been a member of the City of Stoke Ladies Football team now for just over three years. I first started off when I was down at Dimensions. I was originally playing for St Thomas More Girls Team and it depends on how well you perform. If you think you are playing well in the school team then the teacher takes you to football tournaments where you have the chance to get noticed. We went down to Dimensions for a schools competition which is where I came across, well they were called the Victoria Storms back then, who are now the City of Stoke Ladies. I met the manager, Jo Burton, and she gave me some details about the club and a brief history. It was originally set up in 1996 giving women the chance to play football. So I eventually built up the courage to go down there; they were training at Northwood Stadium at that time, on Tuesdays for three hours in the evening and three hours every Sunday morning. I was petrified at the sight of some of them. I didn't dare look them in the eye or anything! I was thinking I was never going to survive this. Nobody took us seriously when we were phoning round for facilities and things like that. We're in the West Midlands Northern Division One. That's full of teams like, I mean we're not obviously in the same league as Newcastle Town because they're in like the Premier. Our league consists of teams like Dudley, Burton Brewers, teams like that. Some of them are joined with the men's teams in their area which makes things better because they can use bigger pitches. The first season we were playing

City of Stoke Ladies Football Team.

Port Vale v. Shrewsbury programme, 1957.

Inside the Victoria Ground.

we were up on some playing fields. We were dodging the rubbish on the pitch, let alone the players. Standards are better in women's teams when they are joined with men's teams because the facilities are way better. We did well last season. I think our success was based on training all the time. We had better facilities during my second season there. We trained on some playing fields that were well maintained down Heron Cross in the summer.

Clare Swetmore, born 1981

Record

I first had a season ticket for the 1984/85 season because a friend had one and I liked football so I thought I'd give it a go. I wasn't particularly interested in Stoke at the time – I was actually an armchair Liverpool fan. The 1984/85 season was a nightmare. It's now known as 'The Holocaust' and because of that season we now hold the record for the lowest ever points in a season – seventeen! So that put me off for about six years. One night in February 1992 me and a mate had nothing much to do and we knew Stoke were playing that night at home against West Brom, so we went. We won 1-0. Massive crowd, brilliant atmosphere, great game and that was it. Stoke forever. The best match I've seen was probably against West Brom in the 1992/93 season when we won 4-3; just magic! The worst match was Oxford. A freezing Wednesday night at the Britannia and it was the most boring game of football I've ever seen in my whole life. The score was 0-0. It was that bad my mate and me spent the second half walking around the stadium trying out different seats. For me this was worse than losing to Birmingham 0-7 as for that game I had free tickets to an executive box with free drinks so I don't remember much about it.

Richard Rogers, born 1969

CHAPTER 3

War Years and Beyond

Territorial Royal Field Artillery, Etruria North Midland, on harvest exercise, 1908.

The interviewees for the most part were born in the inter-war period or post-1945. The First World War does not feature in the following reminiscences. One or two interviewees however, had some stunning photographs of the 1914-18 era and these have been included. Photographs carry many meanings or messages and the period of the First World War remains emotionally charged. These photographs are of now unknown soldiers many of whom probably did not come back from the war. The images speak for themselves. But war is not just about those on active service. It affects those left behind and it is their stories the text concentrates on as well as on national service and the return to work.

The Big Day

In 1938, June 1938, Albert and I entered a competition in 'Titbits' and we won £50. Then in 1939 the war broke out. It was a very solemn day, all the worries of course about what's going to happen. It was a bit scary. About a week after the war started we

Pontoon parade, 5th North Staffordshires at St Albans.

were sitting on Clayton Green because the car had broken down and Albert says 'Shall we get married?' and I said 'What with?' I was working three days and my wages were only 18s a week. We still had the £50 in the bank so we decided we'd go ahead. We got a house in Riverside Road, Trent Vale, a semi-detached house. The arrangement was that we would pay 10s a week while the war was on and then at the end of the war we could sort of purchase it on a mortgage. We went to the Warwickshire Furniture Company in Hanley for our furniture and paid a £1 a week for that and my mother-in-law decided she'd pay half of that which was very good of her actually. We had the wedding at Trent Vale church. The cake was made by Miss Kettle of London Road, Newcastle, the ring was from Goodwins. Photographs – just one of the group and one of the bride and groom, that was all. My wedding dress was 30s, the veil was 10s. We didn't have a honeymoon. We went to work the next day. Our big day was Sunday 29 October 1939. A taxi from the Creamline taxi company arrived to pick up my mum and two bridesmaids. Then another taxi trimmed with cream satin ribbons came to pick up my dad and I. When I arrived at church, Albert was dressed in a very smart black suit and wearing a white bow tie and black patent shoes. He did look smart. His brother Levi was his best man and Prudence who had purchased her dress of lilac taffeta down in Coventry, was also there waiting. Our wedding ceremony was performed by the curate, the Revd C.F. Miles. The vicar was unable to do it as he had a confirmation service to conduct with the bishop immediately after our ceremony. After the service we went to the Castle Hotel for the reception: lunch for sixty guests plus seven bottles of wine, a bottle of sherry, sixty cigarettes and lunch

A corporal of the 5th North Staffs proudly wears the 1914-15 Star, the War medal and the Victory Medal. His Lance-Corporal colleague wears a ribbon of possibly a coronation medal.

for six children. The cost was £12 15s 4½d. We stayed at the Castle Hotel until about midnight. Then we came to our new home in a Creamline taxi. We both had to go to work the next morning, Albert at 7.30 and I at 8.15. Albert cycled to the Wedgwood factory at Barlaston and I to the Hubank shop in the Ironmarket. I used to prepare all the things needed for the evening meal and Albert cooked it when he came home from work at about five thirty every night. I didn't get home until about seven thirty. It was nice to come home to a well cooked meal. Some of our favourite ones were smoked bacon with tomatoes, sausages and mash, lamb chops and veg and quite often Albert would cook a rice pudding. We had a lovely cooking range in the dining room; there was a bright coal fire at one side and at the other side, a nice big oven.

Eveline Shore, born 1919

Queueing

Oh yes, you queued everywhere. If you saw a queue you'd automatically join it and then when you got there you'd ask what the queue was for. Quite often it was for the number 8 battery for your torch, because everybody carried a torch and the number 8 battery was the most popular size. And

An unexpected burst of Greetings, Christmas card.

we'd have gas masks in a little box about six inches square and on a bit of string, and we'd sling 'em round our shoulders. That was common for quite a while when the war started because they were frightened of the Germans using gases. Everyone had a gas mask and they'd got to take them with them wherever they went.

Len Woolliscroft, born 1916

Call Up

We were having a very happy time together, doing a few odd jobs around the house, putting up cupboards and when the weather got a bit better, doing a bit of gardening. But all the time there was also the thought of how long it would be before Albert's call up papers came. They arrived one morning in early March after Albert had gone to work. I didn't feel like going to work that day. Now we really knew that there was a war on. The morning Albert left home I felt really sad and tearful, but he had to go. All our parents and I went down to Stoke railway station to wave him off. Oh how heavy my heart felt as we approached Stoke station. Albert was putting a brave face on things. On the station were quite a few other young men waiting for the same train, so Albert had a few friends to keep him company. The army had been the last department of the armed services he had wanted. When he had earlier attended the medical examination he had told them he wanted the Air Force, then the navy and last of all the army. But it was no use arguing. If one was needed more in the army, then one had to obey. Albert had decided that if at all possible my parents and my sister Kathleen were to come and live at our house while he was away. Much to my surprise my dad agreed to this.

Eveline Shore, born 1919

Odd Jobs

Mother did various jobs. She worked off and on when we were little. When the war came on she, in patriotic fervour I think it was, she went and started to work for the Swynnerton armaments factory. Damn near killed her. She was in what they called the yellow powder where women and girls who worked in that, well you could tell them miles away... they were bright yellow. Absolutely bright yellow. Their skin was dyed. But it faded eventually. Unfortunately she contracted asthma and she had to move out of that.

Graham Davies, born 1930

Essential Work

In March 1941 I went for essential work. I tried to join the police force but I was too young, you had to be twenty-one. So, I decided to go on the buses. I went down to the PMT office for an interview and they told me I was to be responsible for all the time keeping and the safety of the passengers. In fact, I was really in charge of the bus which I was a bit afraid of. The man warned me that if I was on the first turn, I couldn't catch the first bus because I *was* the first bus! We had to walk to work. During the first two weeks I did short fares between Stoke and Trentham, then after two weeks I went on longer distances to Stafford, Cannock, Derby, Buxton. There was a lot of stops and on each trip there was about a thousand fares to remember. I was given a thorough medical examination which I passed, measured for a uniform, provided with a cap and a public service badge number 16520, for which I had to pay two shillings which was returnable at the end of my service with the company. A large leather bag was provided to hold the cash in and we were loaned two shillings petty cash. I had to buy my own ticket rack. I bought a strong wooden one with two rows of clips on either side which held up to forty eight bundles of tickets. If any tickets were lost or unaccounted for, the cash was taken from my pay. As I was about to go off duty on my first week, looking forward to going home and enjoying a meal, an inspector asked if I would conduct a double decker bus to Stafford and back. There was a large queue of anxious people so how could I refuse! I did not know the fares or the stops, especially in the black out. The inspector filled my rack with tickets up to two shillings and told me to consult the fare book if necessary. There was only a glimmer of light in the bus, but somehow I managed. Most of the passengers were regulars and knew the fares and stops they needed. When we came off duty we counted our cash on a large wooden board, passed it to the cashier and made sure the amount corresponded with the amount of tickets sold. Imagine the shock when I cashed up and found that in the dim light I had issued one shilling tickets which were pale blue, in place of penny ones which were white. There were fifty tickets in a bundle so this was quite a loss. There was still an inspector on duty and when I explained what had happened he said he would arrange for the deduction from my pay to be cancelled. What a relief!

Eveline Shore, born 1919

The North Staffordshire Home Guard at Barlaston.

Blackout

People of my generation would remember the blackout. The buses were always crowded because not everybody had a car. On a really dark night you could barely see a bus approaching, but they'd stop at every stop. You'd get on board the bus and it'd be absolutely dark inside and a voice from the back might shout that there was a seat and you'd feel your way along the bus. Usually there wasn't a seat. Lots of people were standing. Every bus stop would have, if not a queue, would have somebody standing there. I always remember in Hanley really long queues for the buses which were coming continuously. There didn't seem to be much of a timetable, they just came! As many got on as got off. There was a wonderful little service that ran from Hanley to Milton through Carmountside. You could set your watch by them.

Graham Davies, born 1930

Horlicks

Sometimes we had to go to the Chatterley Whitfield colliery, taking the workers going onto the morning shift and when we got there we had to park the bus. It was very tricky to direct the driver to his parking place in the blackout. Then we went into the canteen to wait for the night staff to come off. It was thick with smoke. Naturally they'd all smoke their twist when they came up from the bottom. You'd fight your way through all the smoke and have a nice fresh cream puff and a drink of Horlicks. They had a bit more food than we did, the miners; extra rations.

Eveline Shore, born 1919

Fire Watching

Fire watching, as I remember, started something like late 1940 and when it first started everyone was responsible for their own property. Most of the buildings in the centre of Hanley where I was involved had got someone on the premises all the time. But this got a bit too much and went on for perhaps twelve months. We got together a party of about twenty men every night and assembled at an ice cream shop, the old building right opposite the Theatre Royal in Pall Mall, Hanley. That was made the headquarters. We had very little training when I look back. We went down to the old pot bank – just down at Shelton. It had been taken over as the base for training people for various jobs. I had to go down there to pick up how to tackle an incendiary bomb. A man would have the hose pipe in his hand, and he'd creep along as best he could on his tummy to keep low down because of the heat involved. And his colleague at the back would be using a stirrup pump to push water along the line to help him put the fire out. The other – the ways they tackled the incendiary bomb –was by a 'bombsnuffer' they called it. It was like a big enamel bowl with a skirt on about three inches deep, a hook on the top, and you had a long pole, perhaps about eight feet long with again a hook on that. And you'd carry this thing along on your tummy if conditions warranted it, and you'd try to put the cover over the bomb to take the air away so that it'd go out.

Len Woolliscroft, born 1916

Bombs

I remember during the war, going to school, there'd been an air raid the night before.

An incendiary bomb had been dropped in my father's yard at Cobridge and set fire to some crates of straw. That was put out but several bombs were dropped. One was dropped in the churchyard at Etruria and exploded. George Leese who used to be the undertaker on Cobridge Road had to put the graveyard straight again. The graves had been damaged. There weren't many of the stones standing even when the church was pulled down many years later. George had to rebury the bodies. It was a very old churchyard. I think it had been closed down before the war.

Don Smith, born 1939

Bomb Damage

One of our old lecturers at Longton College of Art, she was a young woman in those days, was coming from Derby through into Longton on the train with a group of American soldiers who looked out of the window as they approached Longton and announced 'Gee, bomb damage', and Longton as far as I know never had a bomb. It looked as if a bomb had hit the place. The joke was during the war was that the *Luftwaffe* would come over and say that they had already done this and carry on.

Graham Davies, born 1930

Hospitality

I remember going with my mother and father for a walk in Tunstall Park after the Sunday evening service. Lots of other people from the church were there. One Sunday in about 1940 we were just coming up to leave the park and on a seat opposite the clock there were two soldiers. They didn't look particularly young and my father said to my mother 'I'm going to speak to these two Tommies'. He'd been in the army in the First World War, and he invited them home with us for a bite of supper. They were both married men and both came from London. One of them came back nearly every weekend when he was in this area. In 1946 I went to college in London and we'd kept in touch with him and his family and he wrote suggesting he could repay some of the hospitality by having me to stay whenever I wanted to go to their house.

Brenda Bailey, born 1928

Shore Leave

My childhood and youth were spent living in Edgeware, north-west London from where I went to the usual schools and finally in 1942 to art school where I met my wife. I was called up into the Navy in 1944 and after a few weeks induction I found myself drafted to a naval training establishment called HMS Excalibur at Alsager in Stoke-on-Trent. I was there for two months towards the end of which occurred the D-Day landings. On occasional weekends, on a Saturday or a Sunday, we were able to get a bit of shore leave, to go into the Potteries. That would have been my very first experience of Stoke-on-Trent. I was absolutely appalled by the blackness of everything and the smoke everywhere because the pottery industry of course was still in full spate of production, partly to meet orders for exports to places like North America and which could earn the country dollars. Famous firms like Wedgwood,

Doulton and Minton were very active in providing products for that market. I remember the blackness of the buildings, the cobbled streets and roads and I still have vivid recollections of so many people walking around the streets dressed in either very dark grey or black garments, rather shabby looking. The men in flat caps, the women wearing very often black skirts, black blouses, but spotless white starched pinafores, lace edged which looked very dramatic. The men, as I say wearing flat caps, but again matching their women folk with spotless, white rayon neck scarves. Both sexes clattered around the pavements in clogs which of course I had never seen before. We had a little bit of culture in our training, a little bit of education, so there were visits into the Potteries, to visit not only the shops but places like the theatre and also the pottery factories. The factories did seem to me extraordinarily primitive with so much woodwork construction, heavily overlaid with the dust of pottery production, plaster dust, clay dust and so on. Lots of people were beavering away on highly repetitive jobs which I had never had experience of before. I was nineteen at that time. So that was my first experience of the Potteries and I never dreamt at that time that I would ever come back. I never had the opportunity to meet local people on close or intimate terms. We met people who were responsible for production in the factories; we met perhaps people in tea shops and cafés. One of the pleasures of going 'ashore' as it was called, having a bit of shore leave, even from a land based establishment, was just to get into somewhere where you could have a nice poached egg on toast and a cup of properly made tea for two or three pence! One would occasionally get into conversation with people who would ask my sailor mates

Alick Smithers, third from right, front row, at HMS Excalibur, *Alsager.*

and me what we were doing in Stoke, being in the navy – our uniforms stood out! What we thought of Stoke, what we knew of Staffordshire. So of course it was a meeting from some points of view of two different cultures. We were only allowed ashore for a few hours at a time, like an afternoon into the evening on a Saturday, or perhaps for longer after morning service if it was our turn for leave on a Sunday. They were never opportunities for real socialising. I didn't have civilian clothes with me. They'd all been parcelled up and sent home when I was issued with navy uniform and it was only when I went home on longer leave like a week or a fortnight, that I could put on civilian clothes. People round here were much more used to seeing the army and the air force of course than the navy. I think people were aware of our camp, that we were there on training.

At the time of the D-Day landings I was in Alsager. We heard about them... we were roused very early in the morning, something like six o'clock and assembled in the main hall of the establishment. The radio was switched on and the BBC news was heard by everybody there, announcing the landings. I was at much too early a stage in my training in the navy to be involved in that. My first posting to a ship was to a paddle steamer moored in the Thames estuary which was supposed to do duty protecting the Thames estuary along with a number of other ships similarly armed with anti-aircraft guns, protecting the estuary from enemy aircraft. Their main purpose was to lay mines to sink our shipping. After that I was... because my funny old paddle steamer from the River Clyde was blown ashore on sand banks during gales in the winter of 1944 to 1945, the ship was paid off, and I was put onto a commission course which led to my becoming a sub-lieutenant. While I was going through that course the war in Europe came to an end and then I was drafted to Scotland where I joined a very small mine sweeper and I spent the rest of my national service time helping to sweep mines in the Channel, mainly off the northern French, Belgian and Dutch coasts.

Alick Smithers, born 1926

Evacuees

We took a family in during the first influx of evacuees. Quite a few I noticed came into our neighbourhood and we took a family of a mother and three children. They were from Colchester which of course is a garrison town I think. The husband, the father, was in the army, he was a regular soldier and I think, I've got a feeling he'd come over from Dunkirk because he did come up for a day or two. There were three children, one boy who was about thirteen at the time and two girls, one who was about seven or eight and a little girl who had her legs in irons. My mother took to her very much and used to make a bit of a fuss of her. I always remember, it would be long after, possibly in the '50s, we had a Christmas card from this girl who would then be in her early teens I should imagine, to my mother but unfortunately no return address and my mother would have loved to have got in touch with her again to see what she was like. But we had those and they went back. It was the invasion scare as brought them of course. Then towards the end we had a couple in from London who'd

Evacuees arrive in the Potteries. (Courtesy of The Sentinel)

been bombed out with the flying bomb, the Doodlebugs as they called them. They stayed until virtually the end of the war. She'd been a cashier at a cinema, and one afternoon the roof was blown off by a flying bomb. She wasn't hurt of course, so she went back home, had been back about an hour when a bomb hit the house. Her husband suffered from polio. He was a very, very good musician, a superb pianist. He loved it here. He loved it because we didn't have a bad piano at home which incidentally was bought as compensation for my sister not going to high school, but that didn't wash with her really. He used to go to the library which used to be in Pall Mall where he found he could get out sheet music. He thought this was fantastic.

Also they used to go to the Victoria Hall for all the orchestral concerts. I used to go as a kid; I had a liking for classical music. When I told him I'd been to a concert he thought I meant a concert party. He was surprised you could see a full orchestra for 2s you know. I think he would have settled in Stoke-on-Trent but she wanted to go back to London. The cinema was rebuilt and she got her job back. She did get a job at the Regent in Piccadilly which put me in good stead because I could get in to see an 'A' film, she would serve me a ticket you see. I always remember going in to see *Snow White and the Seven Dwarves* which was an 'A' film. That was the second time round obviously but not letting a fourteen year old in to see it was a bit much. It was the Watch Committee who thought the witches scene would frighten young children. The other evacuees, we used to play with them.

Graham Davies, born 1930

Cosmopolitan

When France fell, and that was about 1940 or '41, Stoke-on-Trent became a cosmopolitan town. We got the Free French, we got the Poles, the Americans, we got the Greeks. All came over to England to get back at the Germans. The Free French soldiers, they wore long cloaks and I can remember they used to put their arms and the cloak around the children and hug them. They were billeted at Shelton. The Greeks, they were billeted at Keele Hall. The Poles were at Trentham Park. The white Americans were billeted at Stoke-on-Trent and the black Americans were billeted at Leek.

Angela Mellor, born 1915

GIs

When the American forces started to arrive the villages and towns were livened up a bit. Pubs were over-full, jeeps and heavy trucks were to be seen screeching around. The time came when the GIs threatened to take over the ladies in Uttoxeter. A ban was put on their activities and they were forbidden to enter the town on certain nights. But as usual a way out was found. Just outside the town was a large wooden fence and we would see the lads sitting there waiting for the girls to go out to them. I felt sad when one young GI gave me the ticket he had travelled from home with, a Greyhound ticket from Philadelphia. He said, 'You may as well keep this, it's a one way ticket.' I kept it as a talisman that he would have good fortune to come through the war safely. There was a great air of expectancy then. Travelling to and from Stafford we would see in the early morning light, heavy army trucks and other military vehicles making their way to the south coast. A few weeks before D-Day my route was to Swynnerton. There was an ammunition factory there. It was also the base for some of the American soldiers. We were waiting for the night workers to come off the factory. The light was dim, then all at once we heard singing and the sound of marching feet. A platoon of smart American soldiers came into view. They were going to the railway station at Cotes Heath. It gave me a queer feeling. They looked like they were ready for battle. On the morning of June 6, I came off a split turn at about ten thirty in the morning and there was a special edition of the local paper being sold in the streets with the news that the invasion had begun. A few days later we were parked on the railway bridge at Stafford waiting for the night shift of a nearby factory to come out, and I looked over the bridge down into the sidings where I saw a Red Cross train. It had brought the wounded back from Europe. This brought the war situation closer to home; it was here in our midst. Two weeks later I was called into the office and told the bus was being supplied to collect a number of wounded soldiers from Sandon Hall which was being used as a war hospital. They were local lads who would be met by relatives in Hanley. I was told I would have to charge them a certain fare. I thought this was an injustice but knew that if I didn't charge them the bus would not be provided again.

Eveline Shore, born 1919

Potatoes

One episode while we were there was the Yanks that used to come down because of the Red Cross in the Market Square. Some of the customers would be queuing for the potatoes and they used to complain that we were serving one or two of them first, but we served them because there were a lot of them and they were big fellas, over six foot for God's sake. You didn't argue with them and they were very generous. They'd give you 6d for a 2d bag of potatoes and a few sweets as well which, I mean, it helped out in those days with rationing.

Reg White, born 1929

The Holocaust

The Holocaust was horrifying, we knew about it but we were helpless. We couldn't do anything about it although we did all we could to help refugees when they came across. We couldn't go out there and demand that we be released and fight our way through to Belsen and all those places because by then, by 1944, it was all over.

Sam Singer, born 1911

VE Day

On VE Day we had a party at the old Burslem Cricket Club and the pavilion was an old First World War Nissen hut. It poured down with rain that day and we were going to have donkeys and all sorts of things. We had the party and the place was leaking with buckets everywhere. After that they put on another which was at the Cobridge Coronation Club.

Don Smith, born 1939

Celebrations

Celebrate the end of the war? Well by that time I was fifteen and there was street parties. I was a bit too old for them at that time! We had a huge bonfire and the local paper shop, it must have had them all through the war, it started selling fireworks. Of course they were banned during the war. When you say did I suffer during the war, yes, we didn't have a fireworks day because you couldn't have fireworks and you couldn't fly a kite. We desperately tried to make explosives, by filling bottles with methylated spirits and having a smoldering bootlace trying to make it explode! Pity Vincent Reilly didn't see us – he'd have drank the lot.

Graham Davies, born 1930

National Service

With National Service I was hoping to see a bit of the world but the farthest I went was just outside Blackpool. I joined up at Padgate near Warrington, did my square bashing there. Then I went on what they called an accelerated course in aircraft engineering. When my posting came through it was at Stoke Heath and I studied the map and the one Stoke Heath I spotted was just outside

Coventry. So I thought that was just on my doorstep and when the travel arrangements came through I realised it was close to Market Drayton. So I was never far from home. I could even cycle home in an evening if I wanted. I used to come home most weekends and I even used to go for forty-eight hour passes to go to camp with the scouts. I even gave a week's leave up at summer to take them to camp close to Stroud.

Ken Smith, born 1929

Instrument Repair

I was called up for national service in April 1949. I was an instrument repairer which involved learning all about instruments, how they were made, how to fix them and eventually when we got on to the operational station, which in my case was Leeming in Yorkshire, you never actually dismantled an instrument. If one went wrong and was faulty you just swapped it for another one which seemed a waste learning all about instruments and clocks and watches. I must admit I never did like my military service because it impinged on my hiking and cycling which unfortunately was the first thing I thought of. I wouldn't have missed it though having said that and I was demobbed just fifty years ago more or less.

Graham Davies, born 1930

Jobs

I started to work again about three weeks after being demobbed. There was a shop down Stoke for the army, navy and air force personnel to go and they'd advise you what jobs was around the city. There was one that interested me that was at Trent Sanitary Works, Johnson Brothers. And what the job entailed was grinding marl for the saggar makers, grinding the marl and the grog in a mill, and when it was mixed with water you scooped it out and put it in a barrow. One charge was a barrow load and weighed five hundred weight. I started for a fiver a week, which I thought at the time was pretty good. It was double what I was earning before the war. The saggar making department was due to be petering out in a year or two's time, because they were knocking all the areas down and changing to gas fired kilns. I finished up full time on the gas plant and we did so much overtime that my pay hardly dropped.

Les Wilson, born 1917

Outdoor Work

My national service ended at the end of May 1951. I'd been out of the country for over two years. I went back to my job at Twyfords but unfortunately my time in the army and being outdoors, I realised that factory life was not for me. So I started to look round for another job so that I could be outside. Eventually I finished up with the Royal Mail and I did thirty-six years with the Post Office.

Albert Dale, born 1931

Vincent

Vincent was a character, was Vincent. He'd done two hundred and something stretches in prison for being drunk and he was on the meths. He used to wander around Hanley, always a well known figure. I've just read the book somebody wrote about him called *The Methylated Spirit* and from what I understand Vincent was often used as a trainee for young bobbies. They'd send young bobbies to bring Vincent in you see. Vincent would never walk as I know to the police station. I once saw a bread van commandeered to take him to the station. Another time outside the Angel where the Birches Head bus used to terminate, then turn back to go Birches Head, I've seen bobbies get on and persuade the driver to take him and Vincent back to the police station. Vincent was not going to walk, oh no. The last time I saw him to speak to I was coming from the art school about half past nine in Hanley and a voice accosted me from the arcade, 'Would you buy one of these sir?' and I thought 'Hello, it's Vincent.' He'd got a little card, black outlined with sob story, a tear-jerking poem about an old soldier. Would I buy a card off him? Just previously he'd been knocked down by a car or a bus, he'd got his leg in plaster and he was on crutches. He told me he was an old soldier which I knew. He said, 'Wounded, wounded, not this war, the first war.' He patted his leg and I said, 'Don't do that Vincent, I know you' and he nearly fell off his crutches. He wanted two pence and I gave him six pence and he 'God Blessed' me right up Lamb Street until I turned the corner by Sherwins and Hanley was absolutely quiet and this 'God bless you sir' was ringing out round all across the Market Square and I couldn't get away fast enough.

Graham Davies, born 1930

The Post-War Boom

Socially and industrially it was a period in this country of great expansion. Somehow the rate at which new things appeared in the shops, the rate at which house building began to take off, cars became available for people to buy... you felt almost from day to day that life was getting better. This was happening in a context in which there were events like the 'Britain Can Make It' exhibition in 1946 which was held at the Victoria and Albert Museum. And there were other events like the 'Ideal Home Exhibition' which was an annual event and from year to year you could see the changes in the quality and ranges of consumer goods and the extent to which factories were developing their technologies for producing anything from washing machines to motor cars to building techniques. So that was all very exciting and stimulating.

Alick Smithers, born 1926

Atomic Dreams

In the 1960s I think everyone was preoccupied with the fear of atomic war which nowadays has receded. I don't think anyone now can appreciate how scary it was. I remember dreaming myself, of mushroom clouds. I think at the time that the Americans didn't realise how poorly prepared the Russians were and they actually believed that the Russians were more powerful than America. Everyone believed it. They all expected to be attacked I think.

Andrew Harrison, born 1947

Reginald Mitchell

We heard I think it was on Radio Stoke, that Alex Humphries was going to unveil

Unveiling of the plaque to Reginald Mitchell, 115 Congleton Road, Butt Lane, 1995.

a plaque in Butt Lane where Reginald Mitchell was born. Now lots of people didn't know that he was born in Butt Lane at all. They always say he was born at Hanley or even at Longton. He was born in Butt Lane and the school was named after him and our children went to Reginald Mitchell School. Knowing Alex and knowing the history I thought I'd go up there and get some photographs. The British Legion were there and I think the Lord Mayor of Newcastle.

Mary White

CHAPTER 4
Work

A double-deck bus on Whitfield Road heading towards Burslem.

The subject of the pottery industry and the coal industry is too large to be done any justice in this volume. The interviewees speak of their connections with either of these industries but mostly concentrate on other forms of work and careers. It is the impact of work on their lives they wished to convey as much as the impact of the industry on the environment. Many sought employment from the earliest age possible, actually being found work by their parents, in order to supplement the family income. Loss of their wage due to ill health, marriage or war was a serious blow to a fragile standard of living.

Red Sky at Night

There was Shelton iron, coal and steel. That was a very big factory and every night pre-war the sky would be lit up. The iron or whatever it was, was put in the huge furnaces and it was melted down. And then they ran the steel off to the rolling mills; I don't quite understand how it was done. But when the steel was molten metal it was run down in huge gullies and the sky would be red. And you could see silhouetted against the red sky the workers, the men. They just wore trousers it was so hot.

Angela Mellor, born 1915

Herb Beer

I expect a lot of the unrest began with the Wall Street Crash in America. The pottery works were not getting the overseas orders and a man named Robinson had taken over some of the pottery works. He encouraged the junior workers to do the jobs which normally would have been done by the more experienced, older workers. This meant that the older workers had to sign on the dole. Dad was reasonably lucky, being a first class mould maker. When there was no work at the Cauldon Works he went to work at Ridgways in Shelton. That lasted for a while and when there was no work there dad then got a job at the Goss China Works in Stoke. Mr Goss started the idea of making china replicas of famous buildings. There was a good sale for these in London, especially when there were such things as cup finals. I remember on one occasion dad actually had to work overtime to complete an order for the sale of these items to get them finished for a big deal. But this did not last. Dad told me once that even Mr Goss himself was having beans on toast for his lunch. We were very lucky, our mam was really a very good business lady. She always found a way to supplement dad's money. First she started making herb beer. She used to wash and scrub the large wash boiler, then we went in the fields and hedgerows collecting nettles, dandelions and yarrow, and from our garden comfrey. With loads of fresh water, sugar and yeast the lovely clear liquid was put into clean bottles and corked. On very hot summer nights we would sometimes hear the corks popping off as the heat made the beer rise. Most of this was sold to the men at the brickyard. They would come down our yard with string tied round their trouser legs, buy the herb beer, then sit on the grass verge by the gate and enjoy their lunch. They brought the bottles back to be filled the next day. On Sundays a lot of people used to pass our gate walking up to Penkhull, which was a pleasant walk. Mum used to put a small table at the top of the yard and set out clean tumblers and sell home-made lemonade or herb beer. About then you could get Eiffel Tower lemonade crystals which were quick and refreshing. She also used to sell small cakes. Another thing we used to make was buttonholes of red and yellow roses backed with a rose leaf or fern with silver paper twined round the stalks. On Saturdays some of the men would take a short cut by our house on the way to the football in Stoke. Mum would make woollen red and white men and at three pence each they soon sold.

Eveline Shore, born 1919

Black Cotton Wool

When there was smoke there was work; when there was no smoke there was no work. I remember I used to go along on my bike towards Biddulph way and the only time I think I ever saw Tunstall was Wakes Week when they weren't firing the ovens. Then Shelton Bar was a pretty good one for pollution. But it was like black cotton wool that used to pour out and drop into the streets and you couldn't see a damn thing. But then it would clear again and everything would be all right. I still marvel even now when I come from Fenton way towards Stoke and I can still see Hartshill because you couldn't see it in the old days. When we moved from Hanley to Bucknall we were the top of the hill and we could look over to see the streets where we'd lived and there was quite an atmosphere over there. God we didn't realise it was that bad and that was in the early '50s. Of course things have changed in all manner now.

Graham Davies, born 1930

Brickworks

In the brick works I worked on a brick press, on the machine. I was the mixer boy at the top as kept the machine charged up with marl. I'd be about fourteen. We used to make about a thousand bricks an hour on the press going for eight hours a day. Whenever the press broke down the boss used to send us for do a bit of quarrying as well, you know, rather than us standing about.

Les Wilson, born 1917

Dirty Job

I mean in those days, lads were expected to do what men do, nowadays you wouldn't be allowed near the machine at fourteen. So after a few more weeks at Beck and Moss the electro platers in Hanley they thought I wasn't suitable material for a polisher and I left there, went up the Labour Exchange again, bear in mind I was still only fourteen, and they sent me along to Warner Brothers in Warner Street, Hanley, an iron foundry. A chap named Beswick ran it. If you were late for work you were locked outside, even if you were walking down the street, he'd lock the door on people. He did it on me once so I went down the park. Unfortunately he phoned me mum up, to see where I was and when I got home that night and told them I said it would only be a shilling out me wages. I was only paid fifteen shillings a week which was a lot of money in them days I believe. It was a dirty job. Anyone who's had a job in an iron foundry will tell you that making the moulds wasn't too bad but when you come to knock the sand out to get the casting out when it had cooled off overnight, that cool sand was like powder. It went right through your clothes and you had to have a bath every night whether you wanted or not. You were filthy.

Reg White, born 1929

Calvin Electric Company

I started work for Calvin Electric Company in High Street, Hanley. I was an errand runner for the first few months and then they took me inside where we used to do a lot of radio battery charging. I more or less ended up in charge, although I was only fourteen or fifteen. I used to collect them up and repair them and general maintenance. And we'd got four or five boys running round the district with a rather large truck collecting these batteries and then about three days later, they'd take them back and collect the necessary fee.

Len Woolliscroft, born 1916

Electrical Porcelain Jollier

I started to work as an electrical porcelain jollier. That's what my father did. The reason I did that instead of the decorating I'd done with Spode and Minton is that I'd been having trouble with my eyes and I really should never have taken it up because my eyesight was not absolutely one hundred per cent. I did that for two years, it was quite a nice job, I liked it and I earned more money than I had ever done in the decorating side. The jolly is the machine you work on. There are two sorts in the industry, the jigger and the jolly. The jigger used to be making plates which forms the back of the plate, the tool that you use, and the jolly is for making hollow ware and it forms, the tool forms, the inside. But in the case of electrical porcelain what we were making were the big electrical insulators. Some you see hanging from the high tension wires and some sticking out of all sorts of things in substations. It was more like, what would you say, porcelain engineering really. It was very exact and although they look huge things, they had to be faultless otherwise they just exploded on test with 40 or 50,000 volts through them.

Graham Davies, born 1930

Twyfords

I started work at Twyfords aged fourteen years and four months. There must have been seventeen or eighteen of us apprentices. I started making small bathroom accessories. Working alongside me as an overlooker was a Mr Jim Lawrence who had been captured at Crete and was exchanged with the British and Germans because he was so badly wounded. He was a nice chap, taught me a lot and we got on well together. At sixteen they transferred me across to what they called the Etruria Works and then I went on to bigger stuff, just making washbowls and WCs, whatever.

Albert Dale, born 1931

Shopping

Weekends was the time when everybody shopped and in the morning were the very posh customers. Everybody talked in whispers because nobody wanted to know what they were buying. And then in the evenings you got the rough, the poor folks. Now these were the folks daddy loved. A lot of the women wore men's caps and a shawl, the cap was always turned back to front and they wore a shawl and long dresses.

Angela Mellor, born 1915

Hotpot Fund

In 1930 things weren't much better. The local councils started to open local church institutes where children could call at lunchtime for a good bowl of soup. At weekends, flags were sold in the streets to get money to cover the cost of this. It was called the Hotpot Fund. Another event was the Green Spot Fund to get playing fields for the children. I was lucky. I had green fields to play in and always came home to a good meal.

Eveline Shore, born 1919

Co-op

The Co-op shops were very homely and everybody knew your first name, especially the butcher anyway. Tom Bailey his name was. My mother always went there for her meat. The errand boy was called Tommy and you could order your meat and the errand boy would come round on his bike with a big basket on you know. Next door was the grocers shop and that had got those wires across the ceiling for the money. All the dried fruits were in those little blue or purple packets. The men were always in those big white aprons. Most ordinary people used the Co-op. Then there was Naylor's. Harold Naylor had a big shop and then he bought another outfitters and made it into a menswear shop. And Bailey's shoe shop was really excellent. People used to come from all over the district for shoes from Bailey's.

Brenda Bailey, born 1928

Looking for Work

Unfortunately at that time there happened to be a mini slump in the industry. I was the last one to be employed, the only unmarried one and the youngest so it was up to me to leave, so I left. I didn't suffer too much because my parents were running a pub up in Bucknall called the Bowling Green Inn and I'd started doing a bit of photography and I could keep myself occupied. I'd got a nice little darkroom. I didn't make anything but I could cover the costs of my photography. Looking round for jobs I was in and out of the dole in Cannon Street. I said not to send me for any jobs I didn't want, because they'd send you for any old thing. In the end it got that I'd lift my eyebrows when I walked in and he'd shake his head. Eventually my mother saw a job advertised in *The Sentinel* and it asked for a printer or a young man to learn and it was a little place in Longton called Hammersley's. I walked in there to enquire about this job and Fred Clay who was the Art Director there he asked if I'd worked on a factory before. I said I'd been an electrical porcelain jollier. But that was the clay end of course and there is a distinct difference between the clay end and the decorating end and when I said the clay end he took a step backwards and asked if I'd ever been in the decorating end. When I told him I'd served my apprenticeship as a guilder he perked up a bit and asked me if I could use a banding wheel which seemed a strange thing to ask a guilder. When I said yes he told me the job had been taken for the printers but he could offer me a job guilding. I said no because I couldn't go back to that because of my eyes.

Graham Davies, born 1930

Engineering

I'd been to the junior technical school at Burslem and I obviously wanted to go into engineering. My father suggested that I go down to the PMT and have a word with them as they'd got an engineering department. I went down and had an interview with the Chief Engineer and because I'd been to the junior technical school he said I was the sort of lad they were after and that he could sort of guarantee me having a job there. But he couldn't set me on; that was the job of the works superintendent and he was on the sick list at the time. So I had to wait for him to come back off sick leave and had another interview. There was no vacancy at the time in the machining shop at PMT so I did three months in the stores which was actually very useful because I got to learn about all the spare parts and where they went you know. Then I went into the machine shop when there was a vacancy. Because of the experience I'd had at the technical school I was able to do various jobs in the machine shop, not just stick to one, serving an apprenticeship. When I was eighteen I was informed I'd got to go for National Service and I was interviewed by Ministry of Defence people to see whether I could complete my apprenticeship and go in as a deferred apprentice at twenty-one which I was successful in doing. I also started at the PMT just at the right time because a few weeks after starting they sent us to the technical college one day a week. I went during the day for machine shop engineering, then two evenings a week on motor vehicle engineering and was on the City and Guilds course for both. But when it came to the exams they happened to be on the same evening for both so I had to drop the motor vehicle and concentrate on the machine shop one, I was the first one at the technical college to get a first class pass.

Ken Smith, born 1929

In Business

My grandfather was a publican on my father's side and also on my mother's side, her parents were publicans. Grandfather Smith kept a pub in Burslem where my father was born, I cannot remember the name of it now, it's been pulled down many years. For many, many years he kept the Dolphin Inn at Cobridge, by Cobridge traffic lights on the opposite side of the road to the Black Boy. Drayton Continental open storage for cars stands on the spot where the Dolphin was. I don't remember the Dolphin myself because it was pulled down about twelve months before I was born. That's where my father started his own business when he was fifteen years of age with a T Model Ford taxi. The T Model Ford taxi [in the photograph] was a left hand drive model. I actually remember it because it stood until about 1948 in the garage, Bedford Garage at Cobridge, which is where my father's transport depot was. Me and my brothers used to play on that. Wish we'd kept it but we didn't! On the photograph my grandfather is the man with the trilby on the extreme left and then my father with the cloth cap on. The man with the bowler hat is George Moss the bookmaker and then my father's aunt. There's a cousin of mine by the name Trevor and who the other people are I just don't know. As I say it was a left hand drive one and when my father bought it, he bought it for £12 10s with no engine. He went from Cobridge station to Trafford Park and bought an engine, brought it back and built it up. I believe it was a 1915 model, but I don't know exactly, but it was imported from America. The photograph was taken at the Dolphin Inn at Cobridge. My father had got a sign up which you can see in the photograph, the Dolphin Garage, taxis for hire, day and night. The phone number was 1320 Central.

Don Smith, born 1939

The Festival of Britain

Then there was the 'Festival of Britain' exhibition itself which was seen by Barry, editor of the *News Chronicle* at the

Taxi for hire at the Dolphin Garage, Cobridge.

time and he had made a proposal to the Labour Government that 1951 would be a great year because it was the hundredth anniversary of the Great Exhibition in Hyde Park. He made a proposal that this was an opportunity for the Government to promote how things were going to improve for everybody and how so many varied aspects of society, whether it was to do with homes, whether it was to do with transport, whether it was to do with ships, whether it was to do with humour, publishing, opportunities for leisure, could all be promoted in a major exhibition on this bomb site on the south shore of the Thames close to central London. My involvement came about because I was at the Royal College of Art at that time and a group of three professors there were given the major responsibility for designing both the building and the interior fitting out for the Lion and Unicorn pavilion. Professors Russell and Gooden were responsible essentially for the structural side of the building. Professor Guyatt who was Head of the School of Graphic Design in which I was a student, was responsible for the visual presentation side of all the ideas. They recruited that great writer and poet Laurie Lee to look after the wordsmithing for the pavilion. He was marvellous to work with, great fun. As the heads of the design team were working into the themeing of the displays and presentations in the pavilion of course they realised that they needed to recruit designers of various kinds. Where they thought they had students who could cope with some of the work, we were pulled in as well. So I and a close colleague and fellow student, Vic Noble, worked very much together on bits of the project. I think one of the most enjoyable one of these from my point of view was with Laurie Lee's idea of having a display panel on the theme of writing for the streets. This was to do with the actual words that were used in advertising and the naming of shops, street signs, road signs. Anything and everything like that and the way that humour and wit could be used in hoardings. Vic was a fairly senior student, in his late twenties or early thirties and he actually owned a motorbike. So, expenses paid by the Festival, we roamed around London, principally the east end of London, looking at everything that related to the theme of writing for the streets. For example, on the fascia of a cycle shop there was a big sign for the benefit of passengers in passing buses, saying 'Get off that bus it will never be yours, buy a bike instead!' As we were going around we took lots of photographs of these things. There was a photographic service provider who had been appointed to do all the photographic work and we got them to do contact prints of all the films we had shot. We selected out the images that suited our purpose and we then put up a rough sketch scheme for this panel which was accepted by the three worthy professors and by Laurie Lee. So we went ahead and did it. My colleague Vic did the heading treatment saying 'Writing for the Streets' which he did very realistically, very skillfully, looking like a cast iron street name sign of the sort that would be cast and supplied by a firm in Birmingham. Beautifully decorative, the cast iron work. We decided to do it as a stylised illustration for the background of this panel, so I did it in the form of torn paper in different shades of black, white and grey. It looked like a street scene and I made provision within that for fascia treatments for shops, signs, lamppost signs and all the rest of it. We reduced or enlarged the photographs we had taken to the size we required and we pasted those on to the panel.

Alick Smithers, born 1926

Roast Potato Machine

I used to have to help out from when I was about twelve years of age, on the roast potato machine in Hanley Market Square. My Uncle Bill used to take it out for my parents because my elder brothers were away in the forces. I used to go down there and help him with the potatoes. My first job with him was opening the bags for him. He served that fast he had to have someone opening these 5 x 5 bags and he used to tell me off if I was slow opening them! He could serve quicker and give change while I was fumbling opening them! But in the end I built up the speed so he didn't natter at me too much. An early recollection I have of it was Vincent Reilly coming along for his weekly bag of potatoes. Uncle Bill used to give him a bag and tell him to be off because if you didn't give him a bag he'd hang around all afternoon making a nuisance of hisself. Like everyone else Vincent liked his jar of ale. It was good on the roaster because it opened your eyes to the people going about their business in the Market Square. On me way home I noticed Palmer's Timber Yard needed strong youths for 35s a week. That was a big jump so I went on the yard and I saw this chap, and I remember his name because he was a friend of me mum's, and that's how he found out me true age. I said I was sixteen like it said on

Display panel on the theme of 'Writing for the Streets' by Alick Smithers and Vic Noble at the Festival of Britain, 1951.

the notice and I started on the Monday morning. My job was to light the fire in the office first thing to warm the place up before the office staff came, go and tidy up round the machines and grease the machines whether they were working or not. Greasing the machines where they did all the shaving, you got shavings all over you and I learnt afterwards that the men wouldn't grease the machine when it was going. With being a lad they just sent me under to do it because they knew I'd get covered in shavings and sawdust. Well I stuck that job for six months, until my mum told them I'd just turned fifteen. So with that they had to finish me because you weren't allowed to work on a timber yard under sixteen.

Reg White, born 1929

Go Out and Earn

On my first day at work I was a bit nervous obviously – straight out of school into the workplace with no such guidance as training officers, careers officers. There was none of that. You just went out and found yourself a job or your parents did. Basically you just went down, saw the guy who was in charge and he gave you a starting date. I was under no pressure to go down the mines whatsoever as long as I went and found myself a job that was it. There was no chance of stopping at home and doing nothing. You had to go out and earn something or your parents found you a job and you just had to accept it.

Charles Bibby, born 1955

Labour Exchange

I went up the labour exchange again. That was a slip up. Being seventeen now I went in with the older ones, not the lads and the man behind the counter, cheeky blighter, he wanted me to sign a form which I did and he told me I had to go wherever because the essential work orders were still on. So I went bricklayer's labouring for Ralph Twigg at Birches Head. Ralph was a great chap and the brickie Tom Chadwick was. The three of us always got on well together doing various jobs to people's houses.

Reg White, born 1929

Window Display

When I was a student in London I took part in a window display competition. We were given a choice of shops for which to do window displays and we selected Lawley's china shop. We decided on a theme 'The Bull in a China Shop' showing that the bull, or in fact because of the shape of the window, the bulls, were so enchanted by the china they didn't wreck the china in the displays. So these were essentially displays of china tableware and collectables of the kind that were available in the market in 1949 and 1950 which was very, very limited indeed. There were a lot of seconds, a lot of very plain ware, undecorated ware. All the best stuff was going for export. But because we won that display, I was able to feature photographs and annotations in my folder of work when I went round looking for jobs. It was that folder that really sold Wedgwood on the idea of engaging me to set up their exhibition and display department in London. That was really the first step in the chain of events that lead to our coming to north Staffordshire.

Alick Smithers, born 1926

Teaching

Well I came to live in the city really after the war because I switched jobs and went into teaching and I applied to go off teaching in Shropshire. Shropshire is a rural county and they didn't need any teachers at that time. They suggested I might do better by going to a bigger authority where there were more schools and so on. Because I'd got relatives over here and I knew the area, I thought this was the place to come to, so I moved over here at the end of the war and settled down in digs at Sneyd Green. I lived in digs for a couple of years and then moved into Greenbank Road and stayed with a cousin until I got married.

Syd Bailey, born 1922

College of Commerce

We went to the old College of Commerce which is now Stoke-on-Trent College and they used to do evening classes in all sorts of things. They started to do O Levels which we took for something to do and then took A Levels and we found out that if you'd got three A Levels you could go teacher training, technical teacher training actually. It was during the latter part of the '50s and the early part of the '60s when things were changing a lot in education and they were after people to teach. What my thing was that we were being trained to teach general studies in technical colleges.

It had got to the point where they thought that any technical student should have a broader education. When I came out I immediately got a job at the College of Art, first of all in Longton then we moved to Burslem, then moved to Stoke, then back to Burslem. I was teaching Geography and English Literature. Then we became a polytechnic in 1969. There was a great rush for different jobs and nobody thought anymore about general studies or liberal studies, as they were known as, until they discovered I'd worked in the industry as a decorator. I was asked then if I'd mind taking over the job of the decorating studio within the Ceramics Department.

Graham Davies, born 1930

Back Home

I was demobilised in 1947, went back home. Because of the provision for ex-servicemen to resume their education I went back to art school for a year. I made an application to the Royal College of Art and was accepted and went onto a three year course there. That took me through to the time of events like the Festival of Britain. Betty, my wife, was on a design course which was orientated towards fashion and costume design. In those days the variety of courses available at art school was very limited. For example the art school we went to in north-west London, Willesdon, there was no such thing as an industrial design course. There was no course for teaching students how to design pottery. Pottery was done in a very elementary way by a very affable and lovable teacher called Fred Harrop who had previously taught and had his own design education at the

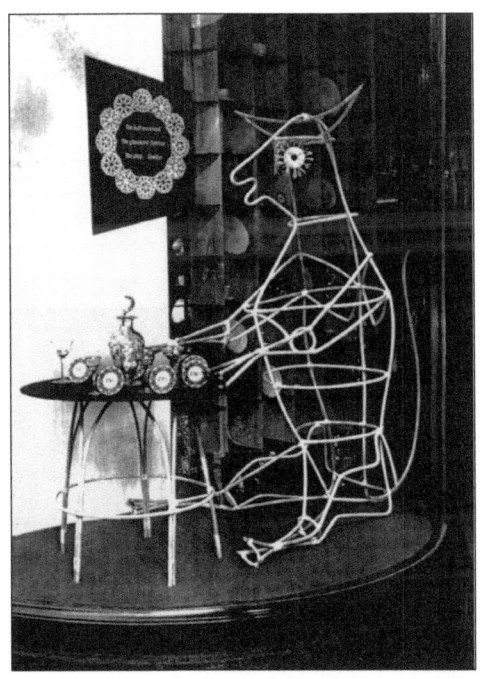

Above and left: *Window display by Alick Smithers and his fellow students on the theme of 'A Bull in a China Shop'.*

Burslem Art School here. He was quite a nice ambassador for north Staffordshire. I went to the art school, learned all the basic skills, drawing, painting and modelling, passed the examinations in those subjects, and then because I didn't really want to do fine art, I took a course in illustration. It was in that subject that I gained entry into the Royal College of Art. It was only when I got to the Royal College of Art that I really realised what the whole field of industrial design was about. At the college I moved from illustration into graphic design and during my second year there I began to appreciate that there were aspects of advertising design, of commercial design that went into three dimensions including things like designing for exhibitions, for trade exhibitions like the Ideal Home

The Technical College, Hanley.

exhibition and also things like window displays, packaging design. So I moved into that while I was at college. With a small group of three other colleagues we entered into a window display competition which was judged in January 1950. It was a student display competition for art schools from all over London and the Home Counties and fortunately we won and it sharpened up my interest further in display and exhibition as a career possibility. So when I left college I joined Sanderson's wallpaper and fabrics in their newly established exhibitions and display section.

Alick Smithers, born 1926

On The Job Training

When I was at Bradeley, where I started teaching, I was an unqualified teacher. Training was on the job. So you taught anything, struggling along as best you could. I was only there for half a term and they then sent me to Brindley Ford. At Brindley Ford they went in at one end as infants and came out the other end as school leavers. They went straight through. One of the teachers who had a class of seven and eight year olds had had a breakdown of some sort and had to leave. They shoved me in right at the deep end. At the end of the year I went to college at Drake Hall, which of course now is a women's prison, out at Eccleshall on an emergency training scheme for teachers. At Brindley Ford the headmaster's office was like a cupboard, that's all he'd got. The toilets were outside in the yard, including the staff toilet. There was no staff room at all. There was no hall; when they had assembly in the morning they used to open a partition between two classrooms.

There were no school meals at all. The kids coming in from Rock End, Biddulph Moor, would bring their sandwiches for dinner and they'd bring either tea or Bovril or cocoa or coffee. One of the main duties you had when you were on dinner duty, you had to boil kettles and make hot drinks. The teachers of course themselves had no school dinners but they used to bring food in as well. Some might bring sausages, some chops, some fish. The last lesson in the morning for the senior class, the top end, was always home economics and what happened was they cooked all these things for the staff! The staff had to have their meal in the top classroom with desks put together and a blackboard put across covered with a cloth. You'd sit around that for your dinner.

Syd Bailey, born 1922

Betterwear

I went to work for the Betterwear Brush Company. I was in my local pub one lunchtime and one of me cousins asked if I was still swapping jobs. He takes me down the Betterware. On the first day on the job we went up Brown Edge. It was snowing. At the end of the day we totalled up what we'd sold and you only got paid commission and the guy training you didn't share his sales with you. If you hadn't sold nothing, just watched him do it, you got nothing. But at the end of the day I'd sold a few items and luckily for me they were pricey items. I'd made £3 on me first day! While I'd been working hard for a living I'd only been making £7 a week which was nothing. At the end of the first week I'd cleared £10 which I was very happy about, bearing in mind it snowed all week and I was only learning the

Policeman on the beat at Arthur Wood and Sons, Longport (Courtesy of Denis Thorpe and The Guardian*).*

The School of Art and Library, Stoke.

Carmountside Secondary Modern School Choir, winners at the Newcastle Festival, 1955.

job. I stuck that job for two or three years until fortunately I met a Londoner by the name of Ron Excel. He taught me how to make polish on me own. It smelt the house out. We used to go round the pubs selling this by the gallon to the pubs. The most expensive part about the job was buying the cans to put the polish in because we used to show them one bottle and sell them another one. We used to sell it at £1 a gallon. At the end of the day you'd always sold about ten gallons one way or another to different publicans. That went on for a month or two. I got fed up and started on me own selling door to door. I had an advert in a paper that specialises in selling to the market people. A firm from Stafford, English Waxes, asked me if I'd like to go selling to the shops for them. The chap's name was Alec Humphries who people in the Potteries will know through C-n-C Supermarkets. He taught me all I know about selling to the shops and retail grocers.

Reg White, born 1929

Exhibition and Display

After one or two changes of job I responded to an advertisement by Wedgwood for a position in their London offices to set up an exhibition and display department. I joined them in October 1955. I had freelanced for a while during that period but I thought a job with Wedgwood offered much more interesting possibilities. I set up their exhibition and display department and was rapidly allowed to recruit other younger designers and we set up what I think was regarded as quite an effective team. When the late Art Director, Victor Skellern, died in 1965 I think it would have been, I was offered a position, not just in exhibition design, but because Wedgwood was taking over a number of smaller companies like Midwinter, like Susie Cooper, like Royal Tuscan, like Adams and so on, they wanted someone with responsibility to the board of directors for studying the design needs for the growing group of companies. I was asked by the then Chairman and Managing Director if I would become Design Coordinator which I accepted. I did that job, working for two or three years in London. But then it became increasingly clear that the job could only be done effectively if we moved up to north Staffordshire. So that was the reason for our moving here in early 1968. I was allowed to bring Betty up for the day to have a look at Stoke-on-Trent and Newcastle-under-Lyme and we thought it worthwhile giving it a go. But for various reasons after three years in that job, I decided to take an opportunity offered by Royal Doulton. So I moved to that firm and was very happy for seventeen years I think it was! I became Exhibition and Display Manager for Doulton.

Alick Smithers, born 1926

Something To Do

We lived in Barlaston for a while and it was okay. It was quite pretty but I hadn't got anything to do! With Matthew now going to school all my children were at school and I was left wondering what to do. I mooched around and went to various exhibitions and I just can't think how it happened, but it might have been at a party I met John Everden who later worked at Staffordshire University as a painter in his own right teaching the history of fashion. That was first of all a few days a week and then I was made full time. I went to Burslem when they moved the college up there for nearly twenty-one years.

When I taught at Canterbury College of Art before I was married, the head of department there was called Joan Mary Nunn. She was very influential with me. She had been costume designer for the Old Vic Theatre in London on Waterloo Road. She had dressed people like Sir Laurence Olivier, Gielgud, all those people and she was absolutely fantastic. She was about ten years older than me and I just looked up to her. I really did model myself on her, there is no doubt about it. My collection of shoes

Joan Mary Nunn in 1947, a great influence on Betty Smithers.

and became head of ceramics at Stoke Polytechnic which is now Staffordshire University. He found me at a loose end and gave me a couple of days teaching at the Sutherland Institute in Lightwood Road, Longton. I was very excited by that with its marvellous north light rooms and so on. I just taught general design and colour and one thing or another for a couple of days. Somebody must have heard about what I did and subsequently I was called to Cauldon College for an interview. I was doing some artwork there but the staff realised that I was really interested in fashion and then they saw that I wasn't a dressmaker as such, but I was very interested in history and the whole thing suddenly snowballed and I was

Betty Smithers models the 'New Look' in autumn 1947.

I started through her because in her house she had a couple of little pewter boots or something, they were so sweet. I thought I'd get those and now have a collection of a hundred or more! I do admire quite an eclectic collection of people and their styles. I think Zandra Rhodes is absolutely amazing, she's so exuberant. She can't cut patterns – she used to lie on the floor and get people to draw around her and sew it up but of course it wouldn't fit because she hadn't taken the circumference into consideration. And of course there was Jean Muir who was entirely different. Sophisticated, incredibly tailored. Beautiful stitching, lovely cut. But the Parisian designers were running the whole fashion business in the 1950s. I know in myself that I feel better when I wear bright colours. I can't stand pastels. But there are times when I feel I have to have good taste and I go through a Jean Muir spell!

Where Stoke College did seem to succeed was when their students applied to the Royal College of Art. The college recognised the Stoke students' ability to cut garments, to tailor which had become a very weak area at other colleges offering fashion courses. We met Jackie Willets one of my ex-students not long ago and when she went to the Royal College with two other students of mine, she said that the other students were amazed at their pattern cutting skills which were to the 'nth' degree in perfection.

Betty Smithers

Spare Time Work

My father died in February 1953 and he left rather a flourishing business in waste metal so I thought I can't give up teaching, I'm a qualified teacher, I've got a degree I'll see if I can stay on as a secretary to the company. Many teachers did this because as teachers they were very badly paid and I did work in my spare time as a secretary of the company. We formed a limited company called George Singer Limited. And we had premises in a new building estate on Hot Lane in Burslem.

Sam Singer, born 1911

Road Transport

I left school at fifteen and worked for a short while at Tom Byatt's in Fenton and then my mother died and I came to work in the business with my father. I went through the transport business start to finish actually and ended up as Managing Director. After father's death I was appointed by the other directors as Managing Director of the company. Father was the sole proprietor. Before then, I'd better go back a few years actually. As I say, after the war, the government changed, Churchill lost the election and Attlee came to power. The government then nationalised road transport and my father in 1950 was running about twenty-eight lorries. He was nationalised by the Labour Government. They just came along and took your business off you and paid you compensation at a later date. Unfortunately my father didn't live long enough to draw his compensation. He did build up again, started another company and when they denationalised he took the old company name and put it to the new one. When he did he was running about thirty-three lorries then, Thames Traders, Bedfords and

The transport yard of W. Smith & Son Transport at Cobridge, 1937.

Albions. I took the company over and built it up to sixty-three lorries altogether. I took a transport company over down in Dorset. We transported general goods out of Stoke-on-Trent. A big customer was British Salt from Sandbach. We used to run down to the south west, not much to London. Two lorries every night used to run to Southampton; they were backloaded with sand, silica sand up to British Industrial Sands at Oakamoor and Mellor Mineral Mills. The other lorries that ran to Dorset, Devon and Cornwall used to bring pottery materials back for the pottery trade: china clays, ball clays, malachite and china stone. We used to put many tons of china stone into James Kent's at Fenton. I should say that 90% of return traffic from the south west was all for the pottery industry in Stoke-on-Trent. There was three companies that virtually controlled the Stoke Potteries: Vic Wild, Wilds Transport of Stoke that is, John Jenks from Longport and myself. There used to be anything up to sixty or seventy lorries per day through the three firms specialising in south west traffic coming into Stoke-on-Trent unloading clay. That's how busy it was in the '60s and the '70s. Mellor Mineral Mills used to have hundreds of tons a week. They used to pug the clay and sell it to the smaller pot banks ready pugged. They were based at Etruria Vale by the Bird in Hand, that area. It's all been built on now. Mellor's used to use china clay in medical supplies, all sorts of things. It's surprising what clay is used for.

Don Smith, born 1939

Co-operative Society

I left school and went to work for the local co-operative society which was the Congleton Equitable and Co-operative Industrial Society. I worked there for nine years and then went working for the dairy at Congleton; it was the Co-op Wholesale Society which was based at Manchester. From there I was made redundant in 1979 and went working at the Royal Ordnance Factory at Radway Green. There I was basically working on the shop floor on the production line producing ammunition, medium calibre ammunition for the British Army, NATO. That was until the early '80s when it was taken over by British Aerospace who I currently work for. Similar sort of thing, ammunition. It went over from a government factory to a private enterprise factory.

Charles Bibby, born 1955

Flat as a Pancake

When I started work I started as an apprentice welder. I started work with Welmac on City Road, Fenton. On there they put me straight on a guillotine. I was cutting a small piece and me middle finger on the left hand, I squashed it because the hydraulic press came down and the finger was as flat as a pancake as you can imagine. They rushed me off to the Royal Infirmary and the consultant there was going to cut the end of me finger off. But there was a junior doctor there who asked to have a look and said they'd been experimenting and could pump up me finger like they do a bike tyre. It was amazing to see it blowing out! He wrapped it all up with stitches.

Kevin Webster, born 1958

Deer

From an early age I remember stories of wild deer roaming the Trentham estate until the Second World War when soldiers billeted there shot them all. I found myself hearing these stories years later in the mid-1980s when I became a field worker on a Survey of Deer in the Trentham/Hanchurch areas where we quickly found that far from being wiped out the Kings Wood area had a good herd of Fallow Deer, led by two large healthy bucks. Both these animals were later killed on the A34 on the same day, both being hit by separate vehicles. This caused some concern among survey members as we expected the herd to break up. However, new animals quickly moved in to fill the vacuum.

Steve Crompton, born 1956

Contribution

It would be nice in a sense to find an opportunity for employment in retirement and to go and live in nice places like York, Chester, Bath or Exeter. But if you go there, all right they can be very pleasant places in which to live, but in a sense you go there and everything is made for you, it's very largely done for you already and I think the great challenge of living here in Stoke is that there is so much to be done that people like us can contribute to. So, we've become very supportive of ideas like saving the bottle ovens, the ones remaining that are still at risk. We participate in this new venture to form a consultative body that will help the city council establish higher standards of urban design with the long term intention of attracting better investment, investment in commerce and industry that will lead to much better kinds of jobs being on offer. Progress is slow on the bottle ovens but I think we have made a breakthrough. The big snag has been to get the owners of the bottle ovens to sign themselves up legally and irrevocably to putting their own match funding into the scheme. We've had significant promises of

The last traditional firing of a bottle oven at the Gladstone Pottery Museum, August 1978. (Courtesy of Denis Thorpe and The Guardian*)*

funding from the Heritage Lottery Fund and the Staffordshire environmental funds for the bottle ovens. We are down now to about 47 bottle ovens surviving out of an estimated total of 2,000 to 2,500 at the peak of production and a large number of these survivors are safe for the foreseeable future. But there are a number that are very seriously at risk and need to be repaired certainly within the next three to five years like the three very large attractive ovens at the James Kent site in Fenton which otherwise will collapse. There are four ovens at the Enson works site in Longton which are owned by the city council. Despite the fact that the council is strapped for money we have managed to bully the Chief Executive and the appropriate Chair of the committee that covers the environment to make the money available. We're asking all the owners to fork out 10 per cent of the cost of repairs, to pay annual membership subscriptions to our trust which we have now set up and of which I am secretary – the Potteries Preservation Trust. We aim to have some say in how the sites are managed once the ovens have been repaired. They are also encouraged to contribute to the on going and long-term costs of maintenance and repair. Some of the owners are being very good about it, wanting to get on with it, wanting their contributions in. Others have been a bit more protective in their attitudes towards their finances and it's taken us eighteen months just to work our way through this enormous maze of legal commitments. Just this last week we've got the last of the legal commitments in our hands so we now need a few months of paperwork to release the grants we've been promised and to accept tenders.

Alick Smithers, born 1926